The Spirit-Filled Life
Founded Upon Grace – Book 2

Eddie Snipes

A book by:
Exchanged Life Discipleship

Copyright © 2015 by Eddie Snipes and
Exchanged Life Discipleship

http://www.exchangedlife.com

ISBN: 978-0692452066

Contact the author by visiting http://www.eddiesnipes.com or http://www.exchangedlife.com

Unless otherwise stated, the scripture in this book have been taken from the New King James Version. Copyright © 1982 by Thomas Nelson, Inc. Used by permission. All rights reserved.

Table of Contents

Introducing the Spirit Filled Life

More than two decades of my Christian life was spent trying to live out my faith through personal effort, which is contrary to God's design. The result was a rollercoaster Christianity with short peaks and a lot of valleys. When I failed, I heard messages like, "Surely your sins will find you out." When I struggled, I didn't rush to the throne of grace for help in my time of need. Instead, I hid from God and used the fig leaves of my works in an attempt to cover my shame.

Well-meaning teachers and preachers encouraged me to try harder, confess more, and force my behavior to become more godly. Church leaders taught the best they could, but because they lacked the fundamental understanding of the life in the Spirit, the church fell back to human methods to 'encourage' people to conform to the life of Christ.

This produced no fruit in my life. Messages of God's wrath and teachings that said I must do more to appease His anger, created a mistrust in God instead of faith. Someone who serves out of fear never trusts their lord. Instead of thriving in fellowship, the one who fears is reduced to a disengaged heart and a mind that looks for ways to escape the threat of anger. A guilt-ridden heart seeking escape can never thrive and flourish.

This is not the Christian life, yet it's the type of faith I was taught. Looking back, most of the people I knew had a shallow and fragile faith. Sometimes, the most spiritual among us would suddenly fall away and become an example of apostasy in the church.

In truth, as people tire of their failing efforts, they grow weary of Christianity, and because they don't want to face their angry god, they fall away. I use a little 'g' in god because this is not the God of the Bible.

The New Covenant of Christ is the revelation of God's unhindered love toward us. It is unhindered because the one thing that prevented man from relating to God has been taken out of the way. That hindrance was sin. The law demands wrath to judge those who sin against the law, but as we studied in the first book of this series, we died and escaped the law, and have been saved from wrath through Christ.

That is the beginning of our faith. Once we begin to comprehend the work of Christ to save us from the law, that merely opens the door to the fullness of the gospel. The Bible says we have been given ALL things that pertain to life and godliness through Christ, and these things are products of God's divine power.[1] There is a reason this is called 'the gospel'. The word 'gospel' means: Good news. If the church is teaching Christians to fear, it isn't good news and has no right to be called the gospel.

The Gospel is God's gift to us, and scripture teaches that He has given us all things. What is excluded from all things? There is an interesting thing I discovered when studying the Greek word that is translated into 'all'. It's the Greek word 'pas' and it means: everything or all. Not some. Not most. We have been given everything that pertains to both our journey of life, and everything that pertains to godliness. We lack nothing!

The reason we don't experience all things is because the Bible teaches that everything is received as a gift by faith. Yet most Christians, myself included, have been taught that we must do for God instead of receive from God. We are taught that we must try harder, muster up faith, become godly, produce righteousness, and many other acts of human religious effort.

God will not honor anything you do that is a replacement for what Christ has already done. When you try to become righteous, you are making yourself a rival of Jesus. Since the Bible says that we are the righteousness of God in Christ,[2] but I try to become righteous *for* God by my own efforts, I am pushing the gift of grace aside and declaring my ability to accomplish righteousness apart from Christ. That is when I fall into the original sin.

Satan's first temptation to man was based on the belief that he could become good apart from God. "You can know good and evil.

---

[1] 2 Peter 1:3
[2] 2 Corinthians 5:21

God knows this and that is why He forbade you to partake of the tree," he told Adam and Eve. The tree was the call of human effort. Become the source of good through human effort by fulfilling the law, and you can become like God. That was the temptation.

This same lie is the foundation of the temptation of self-righteousness. Self-righteousness is not only those who look down their holy snouts at those deemed less spiritual. Self-righteousness is also you and I, who are sincerely trying to become righteous for God by doing our best, instead of by receiving grace.

Yet, the same call given to Adam and Eve is also given to us today. You may freely partake of all things – except that one tree. God has made us beneficiaries of His work with only one restriction – do not try to become independent of God.

But the temptation can be very subtle. **Genesis 3:1** says:
Now the serpent was more cunning than any beast of the field...

Satan is still the same cunning serpent. He knows that if he tells the Christian to reject Christ and go into outright rebellion against God, he won't have much success. Instead, he says, "Has God indeed said, 'You have been given all things?' The fruit of the Spirit is not sufficient. You can do better if you become righteous *for* God. You haven't been given all things that pertain to godliness. No, God gives you the ability to do it yourself."

Countless Christians are buying into the lie that grace empowers you to be like God. Many are teaching the church that grace is the power you take away from God, and then you must produce your own righteousness to please Him.

Then the Christian life is driven out of the garden of God's provision, and into the barren place where fruitless toil plagues us all our lives. A toil that does not produce anything that goes beyond this life of the flesh. Or as Jesus said, "Whatever is born of the flesh is flesh. That which is born of the Spirit is spirit." And the Bible also says that flesh[3] and blood cannot inherit the Kingdom of God.[4]

---

[3] John 3:6
[4] 1 Corinthians 15:50

If this is true, and it is, then any human effort is bound to the flesh and can NEVER enter the life of the Spirit. Human righteousness is abhorrent to the Spirit. Human righteousness is a rebellion against God. Yet the rebellion is presented to us in such a way that we believe the father of lies,[5] even though it directly, but subtly, contradicts the scriptures.

Isaiah 64:6 tells us that all our righteous acts are filthy in God's sight. It is abhorrent to God. The same Bible that warns that our self-produced righteousness is corrupted by the flesh, also tells us that God credits us with His own righteousness, and this is a gift.[6]

A gift cannot be earned in any way. In fact, if you read Romans 4:4-5 you will see that God warns that if we try to earn God's gifts of grace (including righteousness), it becomes unattainable. The moment we try to earn God's favor, God immediately puts all our efforts toward our debt to sin. And this is a debt that can never be paid off. We are given a choice: trust in God's promise that we have been given everything that pertains to life and godliness, or trust in human effort, and spend your life paying an impossible debt.

We have been given exceedingly great promises. The one who walks by faith in the Spirit has no debt and need not worry about the old life in the flesh. Let's see some of these promises. First look at **Galatians 5:16**

I say then: Walk in the Spirit, and you shall not fulfill the lust of the flesh.

We'll dig into this passage deeper in a later chapter, but it's worth previewing here. In the Spirit, the flesh has no power. You don't need to fight it. You don't need to try to conform it to a godly standard. You don't need to overcome your lusts. By the way, lusts is not only sensuality; it is any craving we experience in the flesh. This includes greed, jealousy, anger, selfishness, hate, bitterness, or any other passion of the flesh.

In the Spirit, you have the promise that the flesh cannot defeat you. It cannot rule you. If you try to overcome, you will be

---

[5] John 8:44
[6] Romans 5:17, Romans 4:5

overcome. You can't defeat the flesh with human effort – which is also an act of the flesh. It's God's job to defeat sin. The Spirit suppresses the flesh, and gives you the certain promise that you WILL NOT fulfill the lust of the flesh. This is reiterated in Micah 7:19, where God promises to forgive us AND suppress our iniquities. This is also reiterated in 2 Peter 1:10, where God promises, "For if you do these things you will never stumble."

You will never stumble? Is that a promise you are living out today? And what things are we to do? We alluded to this earlier, but let's look at more of this passage now, **2 Peter 1:3-4**

> [3] as His divine power has given to us all things that *pertain* to life and godliness, through the knowledge of Him who called us by glory and virtue,
> [4] by which have been given to us exceedingly great and precious promises, that through these you may be partakers of the divine nature, having escaped the corruption *that is* in the world through lust.

We begin the 'do' from the foundation of this promise, "We have been given all things," and, "We are partakers of God's divine nature." The very next verse begins with this statement, "For this very reason, add to your faith virtue..."

For what reason? The reason is that we believe in the promise that we have been given everything through Christ, and we trust enough to become partakers of God's nature. The 'do' is to 'partake' or receive, which is an act of faith.

But somehow the church has turned this into a work of human effort. I was taught that adding to my faith virtue meant that I had to make myself a morally strong person. Virtue means moral excellence. Then I was told to make myself control my passions so I could add self-control. Then the list of God's exceedingly great and precious promises was perverted into a list of to-do's, and became a new form of the law.

We must read this in its full context. For this reason', tells us why we are adding, and *from where* we are receiving what we add. Faith is not added because faith is already in place. We begin adding the gifts of God's nature to the faith we have already been given, and the life of Christ we have been established upon. We are adding what we are discovering through our fellowship with God in the Spirit.

Once human effort becomes our focus, we step out of the Spirit, and these things become unattainable. This is why I lived a rollercoaster life and became increasingly frustrated. This is why the church falls back to fear tactics in order to keep people under control.

If the fruit of the Spirit is not emerging (and self-control is the fruit of the Spirit[7]), then we are tempted to create a fragile version of self-control through human effort. Therefore, we must use fear and shame to persuade people to employ human effort. But the Bible says the believer should have no fear[8] and that anyone who believes on Christ will not be put to shame.[9]

Nearly every tactic the church falls back on depends on the very things the Bible says we have been delivered from. Why is this so? It is because the church does not understand the life of the Spirit.

The Christian life does not work outside of walking in the Spirit. Grace cannot be fully experienced without walking in the Spirit. Victory is only to those who learn how to walk in the Spirit. For the Christian, it is vital to understand what it means to walk in the Spirit.

The first book in this series focused on the revelation of grace, but this truth should lead us to the understanding of walking in the Spirit.

To the unbelieving church, grace sounds like a license to sin. The reason people say things like, "Hypergrace will lead you into sin," or "Grace teachers/believers will become unteathered from scripture," is because they are missing the most vital truth of the Bible – our call to live in the Spirit.

---

[7] Galatians 5:22-23
[8] 1 John 4:16-19
[9] Romans 10:11

The richer truths of the Bible cannot be understood without both the understanding of God's abounding (or hyper) grace, and the understanding of our life in the Spirit.

The flesh of human effort can never make your life more right with God, nor can human effort transform the flesh into an instrument of righteousness. The Bible tells us to present our bodies as instruments of righteousness once we understand grace, so that we learn to trust God, and walk in the Spirit.

That is when the promise, "Walk in the Spirit and you will not fulfill the lusts of the flesh," emerges. You don't subdue the flesh so you can walk in the Spirit. You don't stop sinning so you can become righteous. You enter by faith into the life of the Spirit, and the Spirit subdues the flesh, and that is when God's righteousness begins to flow unhindered. Righteousness is God's gift of grace, and once we are walking in grace, sin is driven out. Then our outward behavior begins to transform as we learn to walk in the Spirit. It cannot work the other way around.

The flesh cannot touch the Spirit, but the Spirit CAN touch the flesh. Yet the Spirit does not depend on the flesh, but instead subdues the flesh so that we can use our bodies as instruments of God's righteousness. God subdues, and then we can present what He has done as a willing offering of faith back to Him.

This is what I hope you take away from this book. My goal is for you to understand what it means to walk in the Spirit, so you learn to experience the fullness of God. What I could never do through twenty-plus years of Christian effort, became a natural lifestyle once I discovered the truths of grace. Until this understanding dawned, I was stuck in a faith dependent upon my abilities and my strength. Once God opened my eyes, the scripture came alive, and I went from an up and down Christianity with limited spiritual growth, to an unlimited life and fellowship with God, and the excitement of discovering what God has stored up for me. And the discoveries are as limitless as God is infinite.

Before we go on, it is important that we understand the defeat of sin. I am assuming that you have read the first book, and have an understanding that sin has been taken out of the way. Until we understand that God has broken the chains of sin and destroyed the law's claim over us, we won't have the faith to trust in God's call to go beyond the shallow Christianity based on perpetual repentance.

In Hebrews 5, the church is scolded for staying in infancy and being dependent upon milk, and not growing into maturity, where they could dig into the deeper meat of the word. After explaining this, we see the following in **Hebrews 6:1**

> Therefore, leaving the discussion of the elementary *principles* of Christ, let us go on to perfection, not laying again the foundation of repentance from dead works and of faith toward God,

This is where the average Christian spends their entire spiritual life. They are stuck feeding on milk and in the elementary things of the scriptures. Repentance is called elementary for a reason. It is how we are introduced to faith, by revealing our need, so we discover the gift of grace through Christ. But we are called to leave the mindset of continually relaying the foundation of repentance, and to go on toward perfection.

We are constantly being perfected as we learn to wean off the flesh, and begin to feed on the goodness of Christ. Then as our focus shifts to the deeper things, we stop focusing on all the distractions of life (including perpetual repentance) and discover the unsearchable richness of God. Then spiritual growth is limitless.

To most Christians, this concept is foreign. In fact, most people are taught that the only way to be right with God is to focus on themselves, and keep looking for faults, so they can keep repenting. It becomes a cycle that never ends and limits Christians to the elementary things of the word.

If this seems hard to accept, I encourage you to read The Revelation of Grace. If you aren't at liberty to buy another book, contact me and I will provide an ebook copy for free. You can email me through my website at exchangedlife.com.

The rest of this book builds upon the understanding we have of grace, and the truth that sin has been defeated.

Discussion Questions

Can a relationship flourish, have joy, and be healthy when one person is under the constant threat of fear and retaliation?

The Bible tells us that God is love. Does love lash out in anger against those who fail to meet its demands?

What makes the New Covenant different than the Old Covenant?

The original sin appealed to man's pride by saying, "You can know good and evil," the call to become righteous apart from God. If we are trying to become righteous by what we do, are we falling under that same deception?

Read 2 Peter 1:3-4. Explain what all things pertaining to life and godliness means in your life.

Read Isaiah 64:6, John 6:28-29, Romans 3:20-24, and Romans 4:6. What can we do to become righteous?

According to Isaiah 64:6, does our righteous acts make us right with God?

According to the New Testament passages you just read, what makes you righteous in God's eyes?

In 2 Peter 1:10, what is it that we must 'do'?

What do you think it means to walk in the Spirit?

Do you have to get sin under control before you can begin walking in the Spirit? Explain your answer.

Why does Hebrews 6:1 tell the church to leave the elementary principles of continuous repentance behind, and to go on toward perfection?

Does focusing on your failures build faith in Christ?

Understanding Our New Nature

You have a single nature. Before Christ, you had a single nature that was inherited through your human lineage, which descended from Adam. A nature that became corrupt when God warned Adam that the day he chose to eat of the forbidden fruit, he would die. The tree had no power in itself; the call was to live by grace or to live by human effort.

The invitation to Adam was to become good apart from God. Once Adam chose to trust in himself over God, his spirit died to God. Life and righteousness can only be received through fellowship with God. Once Adam chose the way of death over the way of faith in God, his spirit died immediately, and the ebbing away of life in his body slowly followed the course of death. This set forth the future course of human history, but it also put God's plan of redemption into motion. Look at **1 Corinthians 15:21-22**

21 For since by man *came* death, by Man also *came* the resurrection of the dead.

22 For as in Adam all die, even so in Christ all shall be made alive.

You inherited a spirit that was dead to God. It's a spirit corrupted by sin. Your old nature drew its direction from a human spirit corrupted through the fall of Adam. This is why you were born into sin, and why sin emerges in a child without any outside influence.

As a father, I never taught my kids how to throw fits. I didn't teach them how to hit, take from each other, disobey, or how to bring forth any other selfish motive they had. Parenting is the process of trying to bring selfish nature under enough control so the child can be socially functional. No one teaches selfishness and sin. This is part of our old nature, and because a child is born with a corrupted nature, they sin. We sin because we were born sinners. We don't become sinners because we sin.

In the same way, we become righteous because we are given a new nature that possesses the righteousness of God. Then we act righteous because it's in our nature to do so. We will act according to our nature.

Even when we were of a sinful nature, we did good things, but the actions did not transform our nature, and our ability to do good deeds was also limited by our nature.

As a new creation, we can also act contrary to our nature, but our outward behavior does not transform our new nature back into a sinful one. Before Christ, we tried to curb our sinful behavior to go against who we were, which sprang from a sinful nature. In Christ we are learning how to draw from our new nature to do righteously, instead of acting out in sin, which goes against who we are now.

Now, we don't commit sins because we have a sinful nature; we sin when we fall back into our old ways of thinking. Just as true godliness is uncomfortable to those who aren't believers, sin is discomforting to our new spirit. Christians can sin, but Christians can never again be at rest in sin. We'll explore this in detail a bit later in the book, but the first concept we must grasp is our change of nature.

As long as we believe our actions are what creates godliness, then we'll continue to live life from a position of defeat, trying to find a way to victory. Once we understand the Bible's promise that righteousness, godliness, and holiness is God's gift to us, and our nature already possesses these things because we are hidden in Christ in God (where sin cannot dwell), then we'll begin to allow the gift of godliness to transform our behavior. It cannot work the other way around.

You were born a sinner. You are born again as a new creation, born of God, with a new nature that is in the image of God. Adam was created in the image of God, but when he fell, that image died and remained dead until Christ buried our old spirit and raised us up with a new spirit.

To help understand the work of Christ, let's look at the illustration given in **Romans 7:1-3**

Our New Nature

¹ Or do you not know, brethren (for I speak to those who know the law), that the law has dominion over a man as long as he lives?

² For the woman who has a husband is bound by the law to *her* husband as long as he lives. But if the husband dies, she is released from the law of *her* husband.

³ So then if, while *her* husband lives, she marries another man, she will be called an adulteress; but if her husband dies, she is free from that law, so that she is no adulteress, though she has married another man.

Let's pause for a moment and look at what has just been said. In the era of the Bible, most marriages were arranged. The bride did not choose her husband. She had to learn how to conform her lifestyle to that of her husband.

In this illustration, the husband is the law. The law is very demanding and cruel. What's more is that the law, by nature, is incompatible with the nature of his wife. Or as the Apostle Paul said, "The law is spiritual, but I am carnal, sold under sin."

The law is a reflection of the perfect character and nature of God. But the law is not a merit system. It is a condemnation system. It constantly examines our lives and asks, "Are you perfect, or are you guilty?" Because our nature is of the flesh (or carnal), we are bound by the limitations of the flesh and can never rise to the full demands of the law. Therefore, we are always found guilty.

Just as no earthly judge waives the requirements of the law simply because we have done enough good to outweigh the bad, the law never merits us for our good. It only penalizes our failures. This is also why the Bible says the law silences every mouth and declares every person in the world to be guilty before God.[10]

We are married to the law, and outside of death, there is no way to be legally free of the demands of the law. But the church is called the Bride of Christ. Christ is the perfect husband. He lays down His life for His bride, is patient, kind, gentle, keeps no records

---

[10] Romans 3:19-20

of wrong, bears her weaknesses, is not provoked to anger, and endures all things.[11]

There is a problem. In order for God's people to be united with Christ, the law has to die. But the law is eternal and can never die. The picture we just read in Romans 7 compares our marriage to the law as our hindrance to be married to Christ. Christ will not be an adulterer, and will not permit us to commit adultery. But until the law is dead, we are bound to the law as long as we live.

It is at this point the Bible makes a complete shift in perspective. The law cannot die, but we can. What's more is that Christ has the power to lay down His life, and He has the power to take it back up again. Greater still, He has the power to bring us into His death, and to raise us with Him into His life.

Then we have the promise that He who has died has been freed from sin. Now let's pick up where we left off in **Romans 7:4-6**

[4] Therefore, my brethren, you also have become dead to the law through the body of Christ, that you may be married to another-- to Him who was raised from the dead, that we should bear fruit to God.

[5] For when we were in the flesh, the sinful passions which were aroused by the law were at work in our members to bear fruit to death.

[6] But now we have been delivered from the law, having died to what we were held by, so that we should serve in the newness of the Spirit and not *in* the oldness of the letter.

The oldness of the letter is the letter of the law that condemned us. The newness of the Spirit is the new life we have as a born again child of God.

The law aroused sin in our flesh, and the law bound us to condemnation. The fruit of that work was death. But because we trusted in the work of Christ, we died to the law and have been delivered from its authority over us.

Someone condemned to a life sentence by our law only serves that sentence until they die. If someone gets a 250 year sentence,

---

[11] 1 Corinthians 13:4-8

that condemnation is nullified once the person dies. No prison keeps corpses in the jail cells. In the same way, once our old nature dies, the sentence is nullified. The law has come to an end. This is expressly stated in **Romans 10:4**

For Christ *is* the end of the law for righteousness to everyone who believes.

The law's demand for our righteousness, which was impossible to fulfill through a carnal nature, has come to an end once we enter Christ. Not only this, but the condemnation for our failures has also come to an end. This is explained in **Romans 8:2**

For the law of the Spirit of life in Christ Jesus has made me free from the law of sin and death.

Both the demands for our righteousness by the law, and the condemnation for our failures has come to an end in Christ. Once you are raised into the Spirit of life, you have already been freed from the law of death. And the Bible declares our death before we are given resurrection life. Look now at **Romans 6:3-7**

3 Or do you not know that as many of us as were baptized into Christ Jesus were baptized into His death?

4 Therefore we were buried with Him through baptism into death, that just as Christ was raised from the dead by the glory of the Father, even so we also should walk in newness of life.

5 For if we have been united together in the likeness of His death, certainly we also shall be *in the likeness* of *His* resurrection,

6 knowing this, that our old man was crucified with *Him*, that the body of sin might be done away with, that we should no longer be slaves of sin.

7 For he who has died has been freed from sin.

Baptism is the outward declaration of your submission to death. You trust in Christ's power to give you life, so you are united with Jesus in death knowing that He is crucifying your old nature (old man) and raising you up as a new creation. The law of sin and death is nullified once your old nature was put to death in Christ.

The Bible calls the Old Testament law the ministry of death. It never calls the law the bringer of life. It is incompatible with human nature, so human nature has to die under sin's condemnation, but a new life emerges with Christ that is under a new law. Reread Romans 8:2. The new law is called the law of the Spirit of life in Christ. Romans 3:27 also calls it the law of faith. Our new law is Christ focused, instead of self-focused. We now have faith in Christ, who fulfilled the law for us, and we are credited with His works as though it were our own.

This is why that when the Jewish people asked Jesus what they must do to do the works of God, Jesus said, "This is the work of God, that you believe on Him (Christ) whom the Father has sent."

Once we are in Christ, it becomes a transgression of the law of faith to rebuild the life bound to the law. After the apostles left the Galatian church, religious people came in and began teaching a Christianized version of the law. It was a mixture of grace – trusting in what Christ has done, but then dependent on legalism – what man must do. Then they received this warning and instruction in a letter from the Apostle Paul in **Galatians 2:18-21**

18 "For if I build again those things which I destroyed, I make myself a transgressor.
19 "For I through the law died to the law that I might live to God.
20 "I have been crucified with Christ; it is no longer I who live, but Christ lives in me; and the *life* which I now live in the flesh I live by faith in the Son of God, who loved me and gave Himself for me.
21 "I do not set aside the grace of God; for if righteousness *comes* through the law, then Christ died in vain."

Paul used empathetic reasoning. He put himself in their place to explain that if we rebuild a Christianized version of the law, we are transgressing the law of faith. We died to the law through Christ, and now we live through Christ, apart from the law. What

Our New Nature

we do can never produce righteousness, for righteousness did not come through the law. It is a gift of God through the Spirit. To try to rebuild the law in our lives becomes a denial of God's gift of grace.

From the point of our new birth on, we are a new creation with a new nature. We cannot live according to our new nature without living by faith. Once our trust shifts from what Christ has done to what we must do, we are no longer in the Spirit but are in the mind set back into flesh. Everything is by faith or it is of the flesh. There is no middle ground. We have been given life, so we must walk according to life. Look at **Romans 6:8-11**

8 Now if we died with Christ, we believe that we shall also live with Him,

9 knowing that Christ, having been raised from the dead, dies no more. Death no longer has dominion over Him.

10 For *the death* that He died, He died to sin once for all; but *the life* that He lives, He lives to God.

11 Likewise you also, reckon yourselves to be dead indeed to sin, but alive to God in Christ Jesus our Lord.

Since these things are true (your old man was crucified, you were raised into new life, death does not have dominion, we don't live in the ministry of death – the law, we live according to Christ's life), you now must reckon two things in your life. You are dead to sin. You are alive in Christ.

This is the foundation of the life in the Spirit. Let me reiterate this essential truth. If you are in Christ, you are dead to sin. You are alive in Christ. Sin does not and cannot have dominion over you. Reckon this to be true!

To reckon is to believe something as a fact. It means that regardless of what circumstances you find yourself in, reckon, or account yourself dead to sin. When you sin, shift your focus from sin to Christ and believe His word to be true. You are dead to sin and it cannot have dominion over you. Stop looking at your weaknesses and failures and focus on Christ and reckon yourself to be alive. You have the life of the Spirit, but until you reckon yourself alive, you will act like a person stuck in the way of death.

Have you ever met someone racked with guilt? I once had someone treat me with hatefulness, but afterward they felt badly. The asked me to forgive them and I affirmed to them that nothing done would be held against them. But they kept apologizing. It was a worthless request at that point. I had long since moved on, but they kept dragging it into our relationship.

After a while, it became irritating. "Don't you believe me? I said you were forgiven and I'm ready to move on. There's no need to ever bring this up again." But a few weeks later, they brought it up again. The wrong done, which seemed insignificant to me, was long forgotten, but was now replaced by perpetual, meaningless repentance. I dreaded seeing them.

This is what we do with God. The entire New Testament, and all the foreshadowed promises in the Old Testament, explains that sin was defeated, taken out of the way, and the sinful nature that could not come into God's presence was destroyed by the work of Christ, and replaced with a new spirit born of God. Christ's completed work became a gift of grace, so that you and I are accounted as complete in Him, and sinless because of Him.

All God requires is that we believe on Christ, who was sent for our reconciliation to God. Jesus became sin for us that we might become the righteousness of God in Him. You are the righteousness of God, not because of anything you do or don't do, but because God has given you His righteousness as a gift of His love for you. And all God asks in return is for you to have faith and reckon this to be true.

Yet the unbelieving doctrine of perpetual repentance undermines the work of Christ. This false teaching insures that each time we come to God, we are not focused on His gift of righteousness to us. We aren't focusing on His gift of life in the Spirit – a life the Bible says cannot sin and cannot be corrupted. Instead, we are focusing on the sin God has reckoned to Christ, and buried in the grave with our old nature. We are reckoning that sin is alive, instead of reckoning ourselves dead to sin.

Our New Nature

Do you think God is pleased when you keep bringing up sin, when God has declared sin as defeated, buried, and gone? Sin only lives in your memory, and the average Christian resurrects it in the form of a false sin consciousness. And religious Christianity teaches people that sin-consciousness is good, when the Bible says reckoning His promises as true in our lives should be our focus.

This is why most Christians are stuck in an elementary form of faith. The truth is that the flesh is dead, and sin can only exist in the flesh, and sin only affects the mind stuck in the flesh. The mind on the Spirit is life and peace, because the mind that believes and walks by faith has left the dead things behind. If God has declared it dead, we must also reckon sin to be dead. A dead thing cannot do anything to you. Carrying it around may stink, but the answer isn't to carry a dead carcass to God. The answer is to drop it and leave the flesh behind.

You are in the Spirit because you are a spiritual creation of God. The flesh has no power against you. You can submit to it, but the problem is not the strength of sin or the power of the flesh. The problem is that you are reckoning sin to be alive and believing the flesh over God. But once you learn to reckon what God says to be true, you are stripping the mirage of sin away. Then life grows unhindered as God has designed it to be.

Keep in mind that God loves, accepts, and blesses you because God is love. He does not love you because you have earned it. He loves you because He delights in expressing His love. He also delights in the person who learns how to trust and receive His love.

Reckon these things to be true, and experience the flow of God's agape love in your life of the Spirit.

Discussion Questions

Can doing good deeds change our old sinful nature into a righteous one?

Can committing sin transform our new nature into a sinful one? Explain your answer.

Why is a Christian no longer bound to the law?

Explain what it means to die and be raised with Christ? How is our life different?

When someone doesn't understand the resurrected life, how does this affect their Christian walk?

Explain what the Bible means, "He who has died has been freed from sin."

If you commit a sin, are you rebound to the law of condemnation?

What does it mean to reckon ourselves dead indeed to sin?

What law is the Christian under?

What does it mean to reckon ourselves dead to sin but alive in Christ?

If you reckon your sins as alive, are you in agreement with God?

What should you do when you commit a sin?

Spirit, Soul, and Body

There are many who teach that the soul and the spirit are the same; however, the Bible does not teach this. The truth is that until you understand the relationship between the body, soul, and spirit, you will be limited in your understanding. This is one of the reasons Christians have a hard time rising above sin. Because of a lack of understanding of what produces sin in the Christian, they fall back to employing the flesh in the hopes they can force it into a godly mold through personal religious effort.

The body cannot be the source of righteousness, works, or any other Christian endeavor. Once we fall back to the flesh, everything we do from that point on is a work of the flesh. What's more, when you employ the flesh for spiritual purposes, you are empowering the flesh. And the flesh does not obey boundaries.

Christian works puff up the fleshly mind. Then pride masquerades as self-confidence. Self-righteousness feeds human pride, and we lose perspective and begin to think we are doing God a service with works that the Lord rejects. What is born of the flesh is flesh, will always be flesh, and cannot enter the life of the Spirit. [12] However, the opposite is not true. The life of the Spirit can and does flow into our natural life. But this is only possible after we have a new spirit that can receive from God's Spirit.

All spiritual life comes through the communion between our spirit and the Spirit of God within us. To understand these things, let's look at the Old Testament's promise of the New Covenant gift of the Holy Spirit – a gift we are now in. Look at **Ezekiel 36:26-27**

26 "I will give you a new heart and put a new spirit within you; I will take the heart of stone out of your flesh and give you a heart of flesh.

27 "I will put My Spirit within you and cause you to walk in My statutes, and you will keep My judgments and do *them*.

---

[12] John 3:6, John 6:63

At the moment of our new birth in Christ, our old fleshly spirit was buried. We were raised in Christ with a new spirit that God places within us. At that moment, everything changes. The heart that was once hardened by sin (which is our old heart of the flesh) was cut away and removed. A new heart that is tender toward God is put within us, so now we can enter the agape love relationship with God.

The phrase 'heart of flesh' that God gives us is not the same as a fleshly heart. It's a word picture that the heart that the Bible says is at war with God and an enemy of God[13] has been replaced with a heart that now has the capacity to receive the love of God, and can return agape love back to God.[14]

This is the starting point for every born again believer. Until we have a new spirit, we can't have a heart in fellowship with God. At the moment of our new birth, true fellowship begins. Your new spirit is in perpetual communion with God's Spirit within you. This is why the Bible says, "You are the temple of God."[15]

Because the Spirit of God is within you, and your new spirit is hidden with God in Christ,[16] you have a fellowship that cannot be broken. You may have heard that when you sin, your fellowship with God is broken. This is impossible. You cannot be in Christ and have God's Spirit in you, and have broken fellowship.

You may be drawn back into the flesh in your mind, but the mind on the flesh does not change the work of God in our hearts. A Christian that is ignorant of the unbreakable fellowship between our spirit and God's Spirit within us may be blind to the reality of our fellowship, but ignorance does not change reality.

This ignorance is what blinds most believers and keeps them in immaturity. The life of the spirit never makes it into their natural mind; therefore, they walk according to their old human reasoning, and never know to look for the well of living waters God has placed within us. Look at the words of Jesus in **John 7:38-39**

---

[13] Romans 5:10, James 4:4, Romans 8:7
[14] 1 John 4:19
[15] 1 Corinthians 3:16
[16] Colossians 3:3

³⁸ "He who believes in Me, as the Scripture has said, out of his heart will flow rivers of living water."
³⁹ But this He spoke concerning the Spirit, whom those believing in Him would receive; for the Holy Spirit was not yet *given*, because Jesus was not yet glorified.

At the resurrection, Christ was glorified and we now have the Spirit Jesus promised. In you God has placed the life of the Spirit, which waters your soul, and can never run dry. Not only that, but once this spiritual life is tapped into, it flows out from us like a river that also waters others.

Jesus did not teach this to those who were about to become apostles. Nor was this directed to preachers or a special anointed class. He proclaimed this to the masses at the Passover Feast, which was given to Israel as a symbol of Christ.

Jesus is reiterating what He told to the woman at the well. To her, He promised this living water. He wasn't talking to a woman worthy of God's favor by her great virtue. He was talking to an adulterous woman who had been divorced five times and was now shacking up with a live-in boyfriend. He was rescuing her from her sins and unveiling a promise that applies to every person who would put their trust in Him.

If this gift is within every believer, why don't we see the evidence in the average Christian life? I believe this is the result of the church's failure to disciple according to God's command. Most Christians are ignorant of the Spirit, the life in the Spirit, and the power of the Spirit within each person. Some are even taught to be afraid of any teaching on the Holy Spirit. Then it is not a lack of the Spirit within us, but our neglect to draw from what God has given us. Or as **Proverbs 20:5** states:
Counsel in the heart of man *is like* deep water, But a man of understanding will draw it out.

If we are taught to neglect or even to disbelieve, we'll live as a person with a powerless religion. Everything is received by faith. Any who don't believe, will not receive what is freely given. Are you drawing from the deep well of living waters? If you are not, it's because of your lack of understanding.

A man of understanding will discover this is within him, and will know to draw it out. Someone without understanding will have untapped potential, because instead of looking to God's indwelling presence, they will look to people. They will glean some inspiration from books and teachings, but until they become a person of understanding, they will be limited to what they can glean from others.

Let me stop for a moment and clarify what is meant by 'a man of understanding'. I repeat this often because it's important to keep in mind. When man is used in the general sense, it is like saying 'mankind'. It is a reference to all people, whether male or female. The Bible does give clear roles that are different between men and women, but when it comes to promises, God says, "There is neither male nor female."[17]

The day God opened my eyes to the reality of spirit life and natural life, everything changed. I began to understand that Christianity was not a life of trying to conform my flesh to a godly standard; it was about learning how to live in the Spirit where the flesh has no power.

Then I began learning the Bible's teaching that the flesh cannot touch the life of the Spirit, but the Spirit can bring the flesh under submission to the will of God. Or as the Bible says in **Galatians 5:16**

I say then: Walk in the Spirit, and you shall not fulfill the lust of the flesh.

The reason this is true is because when we are living by the Spirit, we put our minds on the things of the Spirit. Then the mind, which is part of our soul, denies the body's demand to be served and instead presents the body as an instrument of righteousness to God.

It cannot work the other way around. If the body is the focus, the mind will only have a showing of righteousness when it gratifies the flesh through pride and self-glorification. But when the desire

---

[17] Galatians 3:28

Spirit, Soul, and Body

of the flesh is in conflict with Christian principles, the mind in the flesh will begin to search for ways to justify its lusts until it finds a way to obtain gratification.

Sadly, most Christians approach faith from this perspective. They will say, "If I can only get this sin under control, I can be a good Christian." They will try to win God's approval by what they do in the body, not believing that God has given us complete acceptance through Christ.

The Bible says that we are accepted in the Beloved (Christ), and everything is designed to bring glory to God's grace. [18] This is one of the hardest truths for the carnal Christian to believe, because it strips all self-effort away and denies the flesh what it craves the most – pride. We want to feel accepted by God because we have done something to earn it. That is a counterfeit faith rooted in the flesh. It's pride masquerading as religion.

Any Christian that lives out their faith through human effort is serving the flesh – even though it looks like spirituality. To help understand this, let's look at **1 Thessalonians 5:23**

Now may the God of peace Himself sanctify you completely; and may your whole spirit, soul, and body be preserved blameless at the coming of our Lord Jesus Christ.

Let's contrast this passage with **1 Corinthians 6:11**
And such were some of you. But you were washed, but you were sanctified, but you were justified in the name of the Lord Jesus and by the Spirit of our God.

If you read the book of 1 Corinthians, the Apostle Paul begins by telling the people that they are called and sanctified in Christ. He then goes on to scold them for being carnal (or fleshly minded) Christians. In Chapter 6, he again scolds them for committing blatant sins, and then he lists the things of the world they were called out of. That is when he says, "And such were some of you."

Then he reminds them that they were (past tense) sanctified and washed in Christ. So do we have a contradiction? Why is the

---

[18] Ephesians 1:6

Christian called 'sanctified', but then told that God will completely sanctify them? Keep in mind that both these books of the Bible were written through the Apostle Paul.

The moment you trusted in Christ, your unsanctified spirit was buried, and you were given a new spirit that is already sanctified. The word 'sanctify' means to be separated from what is profane and set aside for God.

The fleshly mind, the same mind that is trying to earn its right to boast in pride, takes the teaching of sanctification and makes it into a human effort. But notice, even the call for sanctification is NOT the work of man. The passage above says that God will sanctify us completely, spirit, soul, and body. It is the work of God, and like all of God's works, it is received by faith in what has been done through Christ. It is the work of God revealed to us, and when we trust in God, we receive His work into our lives.

It's commonly taught in the church that we have justification, but now we must work toward sanctification. People see the flesh emerging instead of the promise of the Spirit. When worldly living shows up in the believer, instead of teaching people how to walk in the Spirit, the church teaches sanctification by human effort.

This sets people up for failure and self-deception. When my best efforts fall short, I will either become frustrated and self-condemning, or I will justify my behavior and deceive myself into believing my works are righteous, or my sins are not really sin. Most people sincerely want to do right, but because the church is often ignorant of the life of the Spirit, we fall back to human reasoning to cover up our inability to become like Christ.

Sanctification is not a human work, though most teach it as such. Then people try to use outward behavior to create righteousness, thinking it will grow us into spiritual maturity. The truth is, faith can't work from the outside in. It must be from the inside out.

The order is critical. Being sanctified completely begins with our spirit – which is already sanctified. That is why the Bible says, "You were sanctified." Your spirit is already set apart for God and CANNOT be profaned. This is why 1 John 3:9 says, "That which is born of God cannot sin, for it is born of God." This is our new life, born of the Spirit. The Bible reaffirms this in 1 Peter 1:23, which teaches that our new life is not corruptible, but is incorruptible.

Sin cannot touch the life of the Spirit. Your spirit is hidden with Christ in God.[19] Sin cannot enter God, and your new nature cannot be touched by sin. Period. It is already sanctified and cannot become unsanctified. So the call for complete sanctification begins with our new spirit, which is with God, in God, and where we have continual communion with God.

The next step in sanctification is the call to be sanctified in our soul. From our spirit, we learn to allow our soul to be sanctified by the working of God's Spirit. Your soul is your personality. It consists of your mind, will, and emotions. Your body does not have a will. It does not have a personality. Once you die, your body is inanimate. The body craves and feels, but it cannot make decisions.

If you stick your hand on a hot stove, your body can't make the decision to move the hand. It can only send pain to persuade your mind to act. If you have a strong enough will, you could keep your hand on a hot object, but the more pain you receive, the stronger your will must be to resist.

The same is true for desires. The flesh desires something, but it cannot make you act. It can send desires to your mind to persuade your will to choose to fulfill a craving, but the body cannot act without employing your mind.

This is why the commonly accepted version of Christianity cannot work. If you begin from the body, you are allowing your mind to submit to your body, but since the body only knows feelings, it is a terrible decision maker. Then the mind becomes a terrible decision maker. The body and the soul must be separated before sanctification can be accomplished. Just as the soul and the spirit were separated when our spirit was sanctified. Consider **Hebrews 4:12**

For the word of God *is* living and powerful, and sharper than any two-edged sword, piercing even to the division of soul and

---

[19] Colossians 3:3

spirit, and of joints and marrow, and is a discerner of the thoughts and intents of the heart.

Faith comes by hearing the word of God.[20] When we believed the word, faith completed its work by dividing the soul from the Spirit. To gain a clearer perspective, lets bring in **Romans 6:6**
Knowing this, that our old man was crucified with *Him*, that the body of sin might be done away with, that we should no longer be slaves of sin.

A little is lost in translation here. The term 'done away with' comes from a single Greek word, 'katargeo', which means: to render idle, or to unemploy.

The body of sin, our flesh nature, or as this passage calls it, our old man, employed our bodies to serve sin. But once that nature was crucified and done away with, the flesh was rendered idle, or unemployed. The flesh nature is gone, but our body of flesh remains. When we were circumcised with the circumcision of Christ, the flesh nature was divided from our soul, and we were sanctified with a new spirit which has a new nature – a nature that is in complete agreement with the Spirit of God.

The unemployed body still has the same craving of sin, but it is powerless to serve sin, and cannot be used by sin to enslave us. Let's bring in another passage to add more clarity. Look now at **Romans 7:22-23**
[22] For I delight in the law of God according to the inward man.
[23] But I see another law in my members, warring against the law of my mind, and bringing me into captivity to the law of sin which is in my members.

Notice, our new nature (or inner man) delights in the law of God. It needs no law to constrain it, for it has the same nature as God. But the law of sin remains in our flesh, so it seeks to overtake our minds in order to bring us back into submission to sin.

_____

[20] Romans 10:17

Spirit, Soul, and Body

In other words, our body seeks to gain control of our soul, so we serve sin and neglect the sanctified life of the inner man. Yet our goal is to submit to God so He can use our sanctified life in the Spirit to bring our soul (which includes our human mind) into its sanctified life, and only then can we consistently bring our bodies under submission to our sanctified life of the Spirit. This also clarifies the words of **Romans 6:13-14**

13 And do not present your members *as* instruments of unrighteousness to sin, but present yourselves to God as being alive from the dead, and your members *as* instruments of righteousness to God.
14 For sin shall not have dominion over you, for you are not under law but under grace.

You cannot succeed in your quest to present your bodies as tools of righteousness if the sanctified life has been neglected. As your soul is brought into sanctification, the body is rendered incapable of employing your mind. The sanctified mind has to first be persuaded to abandon the Spirit, and enter the flesh, before it is possible to fall back into sin. Look at how **Romans 8:10-11** explains the ever-present sin in our bodies of flesh:

10 And if Christ *is* in you, the body *is* dead because of sin, but the Spirit *is* life because of righteousness.
11 But if the Spirit of Him who raised Jesus from the dead dwells in you, He who raised Christ from the dead will also give life to your mortal bodies through His Spirit who dwells in you.

Keep in mind that this was written to the Christian. Sin is always present in your flesh. Paul explains this when he says, "When I sin, it is not I [or the inner man] that does it. It is sin that dwells in my members [which is the body of flesh]."[21]

This is why you cannot serve God through your flesh. This is why you cannot overcome your weaknesses and the sins that easily overtake you. This is why you can't get control of your temper,

---

[21] Romans 7:20-23

lusts, greed, jealousy, selfishness, or any other work of the flesh. If you use the body to fight against the desires of the body, you are still empowering the body and submitting to it. It may mimic good for a while, but when the body has a deeper craving or doesn't feel glorified by self-righteousness, it will seek gratification through some form of sin.

I say through sin, but perhaps I should say 'obvious sin'. Everything that originates from the flesh is sin – even if it looks good to our human eyes.

But when we are walking in the Spirit, we are looking to the power of God. We are trusting in God to accomplish His work. We are learning what the Apostles declared, "In me, that is in my flesh, nothing good dwells."[22] Since this is true, any righteous act that comes from a source that cannot produce good is actually sin masquerading as righteousness. It is a subtle form of self-glorification.

Yet, sin becomes irrelevant and powerless to the one who is walking by faith. For we are trusting in God's power, God's righteousness, God's work of sanctification, and all God's gifts of grace. Then instead of trying to be good for God, we begin receiving the goodness of God. Instead of trying to be strong for God, we discover the strength of God. Instead of trying to sanctify ourselves, we learn to submit to God so He can sanctify us completely, spirit, soul, and body.

Once we understand that we are already sanctified, we begin to walk by faith in the sanctified life. Instead of trusting in the power of sin to defeat us, be begin trusting in the power of God to defeat sin. We stop focusing on sin, and start focusing on our fellowship with God.

As we become more Christ-focused, the sanctification of the Spirit begins to do its work to divide the soul from the body. The body is still corrupted by sin, but when our minds are in the Spirit, we separate from the body of sin, and are sanctified in our minds. That's when we begin to live according to the inner man. Look now at **Romans 8:5**

---

[22] Romans 7:18

Spirit, Soul, and Body

For those who live according to the flesh set their minds on the things of the flesh, but those *who live* according to the Spirit, the things of the Spirit.

The Bible goes on to say that the mind in the flesh is death, but the mind in the Spirit is life and peace. The body is dead because of sin; therefore, anyone whose soul is being led by the flesh will be in death. This does not mean we lose salvation. It means the dead life of sin is the only fruit we can expect to see emerging from our lives.

Don't forget the passage we read earlier. The same Spirit that raised Christ Jesus from the dead has the power to give life to your mortal bodies. If your trust is in the flesh, life fades and the fruit of death emerges. If your trust is in Christ, by faith you are receiving the life of the Spirit, and God will reveal His power in you to give life to your mortal bodies.

You are not called to defeat sin. It is God's job to defeat sin. You are not called to force your outer life into a godly standard. You are called to receive the life of the Spirit so that God gives life to your bodies, then He causes you to keep His ways, and He suppresses the flesh and brings it under subjection. Then you take advantage of God's gift and use your body as a tool for righteousness.

This can only work when we begin from the position of righteousness. It cannot work when we try to become righteous. We don't force our outward life into a Christian standard in the hopes we will start thinking differently. We learn how to walk in faith, so the gift of righteousness flows into the mind set on the Spirit. Then the sanctified mind, in cooperation with the sanctified spirit, will exercise the power of the Holy Spirit to sanctify the outward behavior to be in agreement with our inward life. That is when our spirit, soul, and body are operating in God's sanctification.

Our calling is not to root sin out of our flesh. Our call is to avoid submitting our bodies again to sin. If you walk in the Spirit, you WILL NOT fulfill the lusts of the flesh.

Let me reiterate, this is what it means to be sanctified, spirit, soul, and body. The life of the Spirit is also given to our spirit. God calls us to set our minds on the Spirit, then the sanctified life fills our soul, produces the fruit of righteousness, and then through our mind (soul) in the Spirit, God uses the resurrection power of the Spirit to give life to our physical bodies, and then our outward behavior begins to conform to the inward life we are experiencing.

It is all the working of God and is His gift we receive by faith. Faith is believing and receiving in this physical life, what God has already given to us in the Spirit. Sanctification is an accomplished fact. By faith, we receive and apply God's finished work to our lives in this world.

Spirit, Soul, and Body

Discussion Questions

Read Isaiah 64:6. Why doesn't God honor our self-efforts, even when we are trying to do good?

How do we become a spirit led man or woman?

Review Ezekiel 36:26-27. What makes a Christian different than an unbeliever?

Can we have fellowship with God through our old nature / spirit?

Does sin break the fellowship between our spirit and God's Spirit? Explain.

Review John 7:38-39. What does this mean in your Christian life?

Why can't you defeat sin through the flesh (or human effort)?

Explain what sanctification is, and how it applies to the Christian life.

What is the difference between body, soul, and spirit?

Explain the process of complete sanctification.

Review Hebrews 4:12. Why does God divide the soul from the spirit?

Why does a Christian sin if they have a new spirit hidden in God?

How do we bring our outward life into a godly way of living?

The Anointing of the Spirit

The anointing of the Spirit is widely misunderstood. Because of the church's ignorance on this subject, 'the anointing' can become a tool for abuse and deception. Throughout history, many people have risen up and drawn disciples after themselves by claiming to have God's special anointing upon them.

Nearly every cult reverences its leader or leaders as a special anointed class. This was true in the era of the disciples, and this misunderstanding of anointing has continued until our day. The Apostle John warned the church of this abuse in **1 John 2:26-27**

26 These things I have written to you concerning those who *try to* deceive you.

27 But the anointing which you have received from Him abides in you, and you do not need that anyone teach you; but as the same anointing teaches you concerning all things, and is true, and is not a lie, and just as it has taught you, you will abide in Him.

People who claim a special anointing are either deceived, or are trying to deceive. You have the anointing of the Holy Spirit. There are different callings, different gifts of the Spirit, different ministries we are empowered to do, but there is only one anointing.

There are generally two groups of people who scoff at the Bible's teaching on anointing. Those who are trying to claim authority over the believers, and those who want to trust in something other than Christ. People idolize pastors and organizations, often calling their leader, 'The man of God'.

If you search the Bible for the teaching on anointing, you'll find the foreshadow of God's anointing, and you will find the Anointed One. In the Old Testament, God anointed two offices. The king of Israel was anointed as king by pouring oil on his head. This was God's declaration that this king was under God's authority, and anyone who rebelled against the king was rebelling against God.

The often misused phrase, "Touch not My anointed," comes from the Old Testament, 1 Chronicles 16:22. This is the book of the chronicles of the kings. The context clearly explains that the focus is on the kings God has appointed and the prophets God has sent. Power hungry people often tried to kill kings in an attempt to seize the throne. When the prophets were sent by God to rebuke kings and political leaders for their sins, wicked men often set out to kill or imprison the prophet. For these reasons, God warned not to touch His anointed.

An Old Testament prophet was anointed just as kings were. However, for the prophet, the oil represented the Holy Spirit covering him and setting him aside for the ministry of God. Both kings and prophets were meant to foreshadow Christ. Christ is both king, and the final prophet. Let's let the Bible explain, **Hebrews 1:1-2**

> [1] God, who at various times and in various ways spoke in time past to the fathers by the prophets,
>
> [2] has in these last days spoken to us by *His* Son, whom He has appointed heir of all things, through whom also He made the worlds;

That is the declaration that Jesus is the final prophet, but He is also the final King. Look at **Revelation 17:14**

> "These will make war with the Lamb, and the Lamb will overcome them, for He is Lord of lords and King of kings; and those *who are* with Him *are* called, chosen, and faithful."

There are no men of God standing in the office like the Old Testament prophets. They all pointed to Christ. They were anointed as men called to foretell of God's plan, but only Jesus is called 'the Anointed One.' The word for Christ in the Old Testament, which was written in Hebrew, is 'Messiah.' The New Testament was written in Greek and uses the word 'Christ.' Both words have the same meaning, "the Anointed One."

There is no longer an outward anointing, for there is no need. Jesus is the anointed one, and any who are in Christ are under His anointing. All things point to Christ, testify of Christ, and glorify Christ. Those who are claiming to be God's anointed are trying to steal Christ's glory for themselves.

John the Baptist was the last Old Testament prophet. Jesus is the ONLY New Testament prophet. There is the New Testament calling of prophets (See Ephesians 4:11), but as with all the other callings of the New Covenant, this role is for the equipping of the saints. It is not a special anointing over the church. This role in the church is listed with apostles, evangelists, teachers and pastors. None of these are lords over the church. You can see this in Acts 15. The Apostles did not demand submission to the church, but met with elders to give their advice as the church tried to resolve the question about putting the Gentiles under the law.

In Luke 22:25-26, Jesus expressly states that church leaders are not permitted to exercise lordship over the church. This is reiterated in 1 Peter 5:1-3. Church leaders are commanded to not use the church for greedy gain, nor to become a lord over the people. The New Testament word 'prophet' means: an interpreter of God's oracles, or someone who uncovers what is hidden by inspiration of God.

The New Testament prophet is someone God has gifted with the ability to dig out truths from the word and make it plain to the church. It is to take what has already been given through the scriptures, and reveal the truths of God to the church by the revelation of the Holy Spirit. It is not a special anointed class that rules the church, or someone whose own words are divinely inspired. The prophet is under the same anointing as the rest of the church.

Once you are in Christ, you are under God's anointing. That is why the Bible says that anyone claiming to have a special anointing is a deceiver. Whether intentional or unintentional, any anointing claim that sets one person over another believer is a false claim and is part of this warning of deception.

The Bible even states that the Holy Spirit does not glorify or testify of Himself, but instead glorifies Christ. If the Spirit refuses to point to His own work and authority, what does that say about us when we point to ourselves?

My anointing is the result of being placed under the anointing and authority of Christ. I am the anointed of God because I am under Jesus' anointing. If you are in Christ, you also have the same anointing.

If this contradicts what you believe or have been taught about God's anointing, I invite you to do a New Testament study on anointing. It is mentioned in 19 passages. There are three main purposes. To anoint the sick when we pray. We are praying for those who are not under God's anointing, or we are testifying to our faith in God's anointing as we pray for those in need.

Every other passage either testifies of Christ's anointing, or it testifies that we are anointed in Christ. Not one time will you find an individual given a special anointing. It does not exist in the New Testament. Each human anointing corresponds to 'us' or 'we'. It is the entire church that is God's anointed because we are the body of Christ.

He is the head, where all the anointing takes place. We are the body, where the anointing flows down. We are united as one body, not as individual separated from the body. We are separated from the world, but one body. Look at **Ephesians 4:4-7**

> 4 *There is* one body and one Spirit, just as you were called in one hope of your calling;
> 5 one Lord, one faith, one baptism;
> 6 one God and Father of all, who *is* above all, and through all, and in you all.
> 7 But to each one of us grace was given according to the measure of Christ's gift.

Why does God spend so much of the New Testament explaining that we are all one? Even Jesus taught this when He explained how the world of the Gentiles exalts one person over another. People are considered to be great by having people under them. "But it shall not be so with you," Jesus said.[23] He explained that they

---

[23] Luke 22:24-28

exercise authority and lordship over those below them, but God's model is for the greatest to be the lowest. Instead of thinking of ourselves as a special class over people, the one who humbles himself is the one God exalts.[24]

You are anointed in Christ, and God's anointing does not permit any believer to be exalted over another. The ground is level at the foot of the cross. God exalts us as we exalt one another and exalt Christ. I am called to preach, teach, and write. That calling is not greater than the one who is called to quietly minister behind the scenes. The calling is the power of God, using us who are incapable of accomplishing God's work. My calling is not greater than your calling. My calling is to be submitted to God, and His power places me into the body of ministry as He sees fit. If God chooses to exalt me, this doesn't show myself to be greater, but rather it shows God's hand is unlimited.

This is why the Bible says, "Not many mighty or noble are called by God."[25] Why is this so? Because when great men and women of the flesh are used, it's hard for them to recognize that without Christ, they can do nothing. Take to heart the words of **2 Corinthians 1:21-22**

[21] Now He who establishes us with you in Christ and has anointed us *is* God,
[22] who also has sealed us and given us the Spirit in our hearts as a guarantee.

Through Christ, you are established in the anointing of God. You aren't anointed apart from Christ. You are in Christ's anointing. To the church, the Apostle John writes in **1 John 2:20**

But you have an anointing from the Holy One, and you know all things.

He has just explained the calling of God to the young children, the adult believers, and the elder Christians. To the entire body of Christ he explains, "You have an anointing from the Holy One." We

---

[24] Matthew 23:11-12
[25] 1 Corinthians 1:26

read earlier that this anointing teaches us all things, and we are not dependent upon teachers in order to discover God's truth.

God has called and appointed teachers, preachers, and all the offices of the church, but at the same time, God makes it clear that you should not become teacher dependent. Nor should teachers look at themselves as an anointed class. God has a calling that gifts Christians with the ability to draw deeper insights from the scriptures for the purpose of helping believers develop in their spiritual growth. But this does not make the body of Christ limited to the teacher knowledge.

I once had a pastor tell me, "God will not allow the people to grow beyond the level of their covering." He identified the pastor as the covering.

First off, Christ is our covering. The head of every man is Christ, see 1 Corinthians 11:3. Not once in the New Testament do we see God placing any man between the Christian and Christ. Second, not one scripture even implies that a believer cannot outgrow his teacher or pastor.

This is a fleshly way of thinking that creates conflict. What happens when God begins to work in someone's life, and that person begins to grow in knowledge and understanding? What happens when they outgrow the leader? Before becoming a pastor, my personal growth was considered to be a threat to more than one pastor. While I viewed my purpose to be an encourager and supporter of the pastor, once they realized I was learning from God and only gleaning from sermons, this caused me to be viewed as a rival. Though I met with them to explain I had no desire for their position, conflict still emerged. I had to learn to hide my calling in order to have peace with church leaders.

I witnessed this as a teen when our youth pastor was driven out of our church. He was one of the most humble men I knew, but he had a passion for the word and preached with much wisdom. Once he was invited to preach on a Sunday morning, and then everything changed. The pastor viewed him as a threat and began a campaign to bring him down. One Sunday, after several attempts to undermine the youth ministry, the pastor called for every member in the church to declare loyalty to him as a pastor or to the youth pastor. He made everyone stand to vote. Caught by surprise, the youth pastor sat there in an awkward position while everyone was forced to vote against him. He was then asked to leave.

The only cause of conflict was that this senior pastor assumed that someone who showed a greater knowledge of the word was a rival, and from that point on he feared the youth pastor's gift and calling of God. Where they could have been a great team for ministry, the belief that the pastor must be the most knowledgeable caused him to be intimidated by potential rivals.

To have someone you've poured your life into become more knowledgeable than you should be an honor, but the fleshly mind views this as a threat.

If I have to be the guru on the hill, then I will be tempted to suppress anyone who tries to climb higher than me. Consider **Psalm 119:99-100**

> [99] I have more understanding than all my teachers, For Your testimonies *are* my meditation.
> [100] I understand more than the ancients, Because I keep Your precepts.

This is God's goal for your life. As God reveals His word to you and enlightens your understanding, you should learn things your teachers haven't taught. In fact, God's desire is to reveal to you things He won't reveal to me. The Lord doesn't give one person all the answers, otherwise we would become puffed up, and we would forget the primary principle of the New Testament church – the entire body is edified by what every person supplies.[26]

If you have the Holy Spirit, you also have the mind of Christ (which we'll discuss in the next chapter). According to 1 John 2:20 above, because of the Spirit's anointing on you, you know all things. This is true because all knowledge comes through the Spirit, and as we study the word, the Spirit gives us understanding, and our growth is limitless. Limitless in God's eyes, but limited by our own unbelief. And most Christians don't believe in God's declaration

---

[26] Ephesians 4:16

that they are anointed; therefore, they look to people instead of to the Spirit.

The head of the believer is not an organization. It is not your denomination. It is not a church that believes they are the only ones. The head of every man is Christ.

The church is not a building. A building is where we meet, but the church is the entire body of believers. This is why we are commanded not to forsake assembling together. God has designed the body to function with the gifts of the Spirit given to every believer. Since you don't have all gifts and all callings, you cannot thrive without the fellowship of the church.

The church struggles to thrive because we have set boundaries on the Spirit. Whether it be denominational boundaries, or the desire to control everything in a service, when we take away the leading of the Spirit, we starve the church of life.

In a church we were visiting, the pastor was defending his decision not to let certain people sing. He frequently denied people's request to sing before the church by saying, "When we know you can't sing, the music minister is going to tell you, 'No.' I'm sorry, but if you can't sing, you can't sing."

Sometimes the most worshipful songs come from the voice of someone who can't hold a note. The Bible says to make a joyful noise, not a professional performance. If someone's heart is filled with praise, they should sing. Or as James 5:13 says, "If anyone among you is cheerful, let him sing." We are sharing our faith with one another, not showing off our talents. There is a place for talent, but it is not the measure of our worthiness to follow the Spirit.

Similarly, I was once asked to teach a class at a church. The director said he recognized God's calling, and wanted me to teach. As we discussed, he made it clear that I had to only teach what was in the denomination distributed Sunday School book. A book that often skewed passages to fit the denominational line, but clearly didn't fit the scripture.

I shared my concerns with the book and though he agreed that they often pushed their agendas by bending the meaning of scripture, he also said, "The material from our organization is safe.

I know I can trust what is being handed down. I'm concerned that if we let people teach on their own, they might teach things we don't agree with."

After a lengthy discussion, I turned down the offer. I asked if he believed God had called me. He said he did. Then I read from Ephesians 4 where God appointed some to be teachers for the equipping of the saints for ministry. Then I read 2 Timothy 3:17 where the word equips us completely for every good work. I asked, "Do you believe the Lord equips the one He calls?" He said he did, but in truth he didn't. He was unwilling to allow any teaching outside of the denominational material.

As we discussed, I asked if he saw maturity developing in the lives of those who stayed in the safe material. Was there more maturity in the church today than there was twenty years ago? Did he witness anyone grow into a deep faith through this material.

Though he acknowledged most longtime Christians were not maturing even after decades of studying this material, he was unwilling to budge from his safe position.

In Proverbs 14:4, the Bible says, "Where there are no oxen, the stall is clean, but there is much increase by the strength of the ox." In many ways, this applies to our Christian walk. If we take the safe, squeaky-clean way, we won't have to do much work, but there is no increase.

In matters of doctrine, the church wants to have a safe, noncontroversial doctrinal statement. We don't want the trouble of someone raising questions, and having to hash out scriptures, and question our own understanding. It's much easier to build up walls and keep questions out. But there is no fruit in insulating our doctrines. There is much increase to gain when we allow questions to be asked and ideas to be explored. The person with a superficial knowledge may be intimidated by challenges to pet beliefs, but the Bible is a goldmine of discoveries waiting for a prospector.

A question we should ask ourselves is, are we seeking the depths of God, or are we trying to build a safe stall that is comfortable and creates apathy? Are we driving away prospectors?

Or are we willing to dig in with them, search the scriptures, and find out if what we are being told is true?

The Bible says, "No other foundation can be laid, than that which has been laid, which is Jesus Christ."[27] If we understand the foundation of Christ and how His finished work is how we receive God's purposes, then we can measure every claim of truth against our solid foundation. From here, there is no limit to what God desires to reveal to us and lay upon the foundation of Christ in our lives.

Regardless of the denomination, the average Christian will learn everything they will ever know within three years of attending church. Most churches rehash the same safe doctrines, mix and match previously taught ideas, but never go beyond the surface. As a result, the church is filled with superficial Christians who have long since stopped growing. When a tree stops growing, it begins to die. The same is true in faith. When we stop growing, we don't stay strong, but we begin to die back. If someone recognizes they are feeling dead spiritually, they may grow back to where they were, but soon that growth dies back again. No one can flourish by being limited to the safe waters of the spiritual kiddie pool.

We are limiting the Spirit and preventing people from wandering into uncontrolled waters, yet we pray, "Lord have your way." God does not operate within our boundaries. He is either Lord, or we are excluding ourselves from His work and the revelation of the Spirit.

It's okay if someone is wrong. Those who are living in the anointing of the Spirit are not intimidated by new concepts. We must be like the Bereans, take what is being taught and search the scriptures to see if what we are being told is true.[28] When people can share what God is showing them, it can become a joyful discovery of the word.

We all bring misconceptions to our studies and personal beliefs cloud our understanding. But when ideas can be freely explored,

---

[27] 1 Corinthians 3:11
[28] Acts 17:10-11

misconceptions fall away and we will either learn something new, or we will have the opportunity to expound the way of truth more accurately.

One of the great missionaries of the early church was Apollos. God worked in this man's life to reveal much in scripture, but there were some missing key doctrines that limited his understanding. In Acts 18, a couple named Priscilla and Aquila heard him teaching. He still had some Old Covenant theology that confused his teaching. Yet this couple had enough spiritual maturity to recognize God's working in Apollos' life. Instead of scolding him, as the fleshly-minded church likes to do today, they invited him into their fellowship. They praised the fact he was mighty in the word, and used this as an opportunity to explain the way of truth more perfectly.

This discipling couple then faded from the pages of scripture, but the man they invested love and truth into became a key figure in starting churches. The Apostle Paul counted him as a peer in ministry and said, "I planted, Apollos watered, but God gave the increase." It began with two people who supported a teacher, even though his doctrine wasn't accurate in every area. They invested instead of viewing him as a rival. They encouraged him to grow in the scriptures, instead of knocking him down for is lack of understanding.

God revealed to Priscilla and Aquila what He did not reveal to Apollos. God used Apollos in ways that excelled above his teachers. But they are all one body with the same mission.

When our doctrines are treated as though we are infallible, we'll be intimidated by ideas that stretch our comfort zone, and will feel the need to stamp out questions, rather than exploring them. This is also why obeying the Bible's command to study is vital. Look at **2 Timothy 2:15-16**

[15] Be diligent to present yourself approved to God, a worker who does not need to be ashamed, rightly dividing the word of truth.

[16] But shun profane *and* idle babblings, for they will increase to more ungodliness.

Let's look at profane and idle babblings first. Profane means common things, something that is not holy. It is a worldly philosophy. Idle babblings means useless talking or fruitless discussions.

If we don't know how to rightly divide the truth, we won't know how to explore ideas and reconcile them to scripture. A person who doesn't know the word is not in a position to resolve ideas and reconcile them to the word. That is when the discussion takes on a worldly flavor, and then opinions, politics, and personal philosophies are placed on par with scripture. This is when the study of the word falls into confusion. It is not the willingness to discuss that creates confusion, but the lack of understanding of the word. And this only comes with diligent study.

Staying in safe waters does not produce clarity. It keeps people from diligently studying the word, and this makes people more vulnerable to error than it does to protect them.

Don't underestimate the Spirit. Through prayer and study, seek understanding through the word. Read quantity so you can get the big picture, and quality so you can meditate on passages as you let the Spirit give you understanding. Keep in mind, Jesus said the Spirit would bring back to remembrance the things He taught His apostles. As we study what the Spirit revealed to the apostles, during our times of seeking, He will bring these passages to our minds as well. That is when you begin to see how one passage complements another to paint a clearer picture.

Without study, we are limiting what the Spirit has to bring to remembrance. I can't remember what I have not read. Though God can work around my limitations, God does not bless apathy. Seek God through the word. Trust in the fact that you are under Christ's anointing, and He has the power to give you understanding. Don't make Bible study a duty, but a time of discovery. Expect God's revelation as you study in faith.

Discussion Questions

Read 1 John 2:20, 26-27. John 14:26. What does the anointing of the Spirit give to the believer in these passages?

To whom is this promise given?

Compare Hebrews 1:1-2 to John 14:26. Did the revelation of the Spirit to the apostles present new teachings that did not originate through Christ?

Read Revelation 1:1. If the purpose of the New Testament is the revelation of Christ, what should New Testament prophets be proclaiming?

Read Mark 10:42-45. Are Jesus' apostles made rulers over the church? What about church leaders today?

Read James 5:14-15. Why are we called to anoint the sick?

Review Psalm 119:99-100. Can God give someone more understanding than those who teach them?

Do church leaders have to be the most knowledgeable?

If someone has more knowledge, does this qualify them for leadership?

Which equips Christians with truth, being sheltered from varying ideas, or exploring them through scripture?

Will our beliefs change as we go deeper in our Bible studies?

Is that a good thing or not? Explain your answer.

The Mind of Christ

In a Bible study, a teacher led a carefully guided lesson. After reading a scripture, a discussion began. The man beside me poked his finger at the bottom of his study Bible and said, "My commentary says this," and went on to read a blurb about the scripture.

It was a scripture rich with truth, most of which was untapped from his commentary Bible, so I probed him. "What do you see in that passage? When you read it, what does God reveal to you?"

He tapped the bottom of the page and said, "The notes say," and he went on to read it again.

After probing a little more but not getting my point across, I said, "Cover the notes for a moment and reread the passage. Then tell me what the Spirit is revealing to you."

At this point, the man became indignant. "Who am I to interpret? Who are you and I to question what these scholars have written?"

This is the attitude of most people. The experts are the trustworthy source, not the Spirit. Of course, people don't stop to realize that they are turning from the Spirit and trusting in men, but it is God who said, "Cursed is the man who trusts in man," [29] and "You don't need any man to teach you. The Spirit teaches you all things, yes the deep things of God." [30]

It is Jesus who said that God has, "Hidden these things from the wise and prudent, and has revealed them to the babes." [31] In other words, God doesn't pick the scholars with the PHDs as the ones He uses to unveil the truth of the word. He can use educated men, but they also must become humble in spirit. The babes are those who are looking to God for the Spirit's provision, and these are the ones who discover the depths of truth. But even the babe has to trust in

---

[29] Jeremiah 17:5
[30] 1 John 2:27
[31] Matthew 11:25

the source of all truth. Those who shun the Spirit and only look to man will only get what man can reveal.

When the apostles of Jesus were being examined by the courts, the educated rulers could not defeat the words of the apostles. They marveled that these uneducated and untrained men could have such wisdom, and they concluded they must have been with Jesus.[32]

The reason God doesn't reveal the deep truths of His word to many great and educated men is because knowledge puffs up. As the natural mind is puffed up, people begin trusting in their own wisdom and never learn to seek the true wisdom, which only comes from the revelation of God. Knowledge without revelation is merely Christianized philosophy. It has little value outside of this world. The Bible lays the groundwork for receiving revelation knowledge in **Proverbs 2:3-9**

[3] Yes, if you cry out for discernment, *And* lift up your voice for understanding,

[4] If you seek her as silver, And search for her as *for* hidden treasures;

[5] Then you will understand the fear of the LORD, And find the knowledge of God.

[6] For the LORD gives wisdom; From His mouth *come* knowledge and understanding;

[7] He stores up sound wisdom for the upright; *He is* a shield to those who walk uprightly;

[8] He guards the paths of justice, And preserves the way of His saints.

[9] Then you will understand righteousness and justice, Equity *and* every good path.

Do you realize that you have these promises within your grasp? These remain hidden to those who lean upon their own wisdom, but God eagerly waits to reveal these things to those who seek for the wisdom that only comes from the Spirit. It's not given to those who trust in their own education. It's not given to those who trust

---

[32] Acts 4:13

in scholars and commentators. We can glean from the works of others, but true revelation knowledge only comes to those who fulfill the above passage.

An obedient teacher will reveal what God is revealing to them, with the intention of guiding others into the same source of true knowledge. God's calling of teaching and preaching is not to create dependents upon the teacher. It is to equip the saints so they become ministers. Each Christian is a minister to the church body, and a witness of God's love to the world. We become effective ministers when we learn to seek and experience firsthand revelation, and then seek to pass on what we are learning to others.

Also note, the above promise is also not given to the apathetic Christian. In the book of James, we are told that if we lack wisdom, let us ask of God, who gives to all men liberally.[33] This is not an apathetic and faithless prayer. It isn't merely asking for God and shrugging off our disappointment when it doesn't fall into our lap.

We ask as we have seen in Proverbs 2 above. We ask with fervent praying, crying out for these things, seeking with our whole heart, and diligently pursuing these promises. If you know this is yours, you will ask, and then start pursuing, knowing God will answer. You will seek, knowing God has stored these things up for you to find. And when you find, you'll keep digging, knowing that the deeper you dig, the more you find. The seeking should never stop. You only stop receiving when you stop seeking.

The Lord gives wisdom. Out of His mouth, which is the word of God, He has provided knowledge and understanding. To the natural mind, knowledge puffs up, but to the mind blessed with God's wisdom, knowledge produces understanding.

Do you truly believe God's word? Set aside all distractions and seek God's wisdom, knowledge, and understanding. First learn how to receive from God, and then you will learn how to glean from commentaries, teachings, and preaching. We have it backwards. Most Christians look at teachers as the main source of understanding, and their own Bible study as a supplement. The word is your spiritual food, and teachings are the supplement.

---

[33] James 1:5

The milk of the word is the teachings we receive from others. A new believer is first fed the word by teachers, but as a Christian matures, they should start learning how to feed themselves. Then we glean from teaching, but are not dependent upon a teacher.

If you are in Christ, you have the Holy Spirit within you. He is your teacher. Through the Spirit, you have been given all things that pertain to life and godliness. You lack nothing. If you see a lack in your ability to draw understanding from the word, this is the evidence you have not yet learned to seek and trust in the Spirit. You have the promise that when you diligently seek, God abundantly reveals. And this promise is cemented with another promise, "Then you will understand righteousness, equity, justice, and EVERY good path! Let's explore a little deeper. Look now at **1 Corinthians 2:14-16**

14 But the natural man does not receive the things of the Spirit of God, for they are foolishness to him; nor can he know *them*, because they are spiritually discerned.
15 But he who is spiritual judges all things, yet he himself is *rightly* judged by no one.
16 For "who has known the mind of the LORD that he may instruct Him?" But we have the mind of Christ.

The natural mind is incapable of receiving or understanding the things of the Spirit. This means that if you are studying with the mere intellect, you can never get beyond the surface of the word. Even the natural mind can understand principles that apply to the natural. Don't steal, kill, or commit blatant sins. Do good, give to others, and do acts of kindness. Christian or not, many of the elementary things can be understood, but not the things that come by revelation.

Don't think the phrase, "the natural mind," only applies to unbelievers. Christians are just as capable of operating in the natural as non-Christians. The world cannot receive the things of the Spirit, nor can the carnally minded Christian. We study with the expectation of revelation as we seek God through His word. We must learn to study in the Spirit, not according to the flesh.

You have the mind of Christ. Anyone who has the Spirit within them has the mind of Christ. The mind of Christ is of the Holy Spirit. This is affirmed in a passage we studied earlier. Let's review **1 John 2:20**

But you have an anointing from the Holy One, and you know all things.

You have the mind of Christ? You know all things? How is this possible if we are so limited in our understanding? These things are true because the source of all knowledge and understanding has taken up residence within us, and has communion with our spirit. Of course, this is the Holy Spirit. Let's bring in another passage to continue painting the picture of this amazing truth. Look now at **1 Corinthians 2:9-11**

9 But as it is written: "Eye has not seen, nor ear heard, Nor have entered into the heart of man The things which God has prepared for those who love Him."

10 But God has revealed *them* to us through His Spirit. For the Spirit searches all things, yes, the deep things of God.

11 For what man knows the things of a man except the spirit of the man which is in him? Even so no one knows the things of God except the Spirit of God.

Once again, the scripture is reiterating the fact that the human intellect can't know or comprehend the things God has prepared for those who love Him. This is not the promise of heaven. Let me emphasize this again. This promise is not speaking of heaven. Indeed, God has prepared many treasures for us in heaven, but look at the context.

The natural mind cannot see, hear, nor imagine the things God has prepared for us. This is what Proverbs 2 is speaking of. God has stored up treasures for you to find now, and the more you seek, the more you discover. These are treasures the world cannot receive. These are the treasures the naturally minded Christian also cannot see, hear, or imagine.

The promise to the Christian is, "But God HAS (past tense) revealed them to us through His Spirit." The natural mind can only know the things of man, but cannot know the things of God. Only the Spirit of God can know the deep things of God. The Spirit searches the deep things of God for the purpose of revealing them to us. I say 'to reveal', but that is to reveal to our human understanding that which has already been revealed to our spirit, which is always a partaker of God's divine nature. [34]

Keep in mind that our spirit is in constant fellowship with God, hidden in Christ in God. [35] God is always inviting us to dive deep into the things of the Spirit, but the limitlessness of our spirit man is hindered by the limits of our natural mind. What has already been given to us in the Spirit has to be sought out through our mind. When our mind is in the Spirit, we can explore the deeper revelations of the word. Or as the Bible states in **Proverbs 20:5**

Counsel in the heart of man *is like* deep water, But a man of understanding will draw it out.

Notice that the counsel is already in our heart, which is referring to our inner man, or spirit man. It's our new spirit spoken of in 2 Corinthians 5:17 and Ezekiel 36:26-27. The Christian who is living by faith will learn to draw the counsel of God's Spirit out of the deep places in our heart, so we can gain understanding. It's the same promise of understanding given to those who diligently seek God through His word.

Something has to draw understanding from our spirit in order to reveal it to our natural mind. That is the work of the Holy Spirit. It is the promise that the Spirit brings the word back to our minds, guides us into all truth, and teaches us. The Spirit is called our counselor, and He is the flow of living waters we are drawing from. [36]

As we seek God through His word, meditate on the word, pray for understanding, and operate in faith, the Spirit begins revealing

---

[34] 2 Peter 1:3-4
[35] Colossians 3:3
[36] John 7:38-39

to our natural mind what is always being revealed in our spirit. This is what is meant by revelation knowledge. It is the Spirit taking our knowledge of the word and revealing the deep truths that the human mind cannot understand or receive.

If the natural mind can't receive it, then the Spirit cannot reveal it. If our minds are in the natural, God rarely gives revelation, for if He did, it wouldn't profit us, since we are not in a state that is capable of applying it by faith.

This is where most Christians spend their entire lives. This is not only true for our generation. The book of Hebrews criticizes the church by saying, "By this time you ought to be teachers, but you are in need of someone teaching you the basic principles of God again."

It does not have to be this way. God does not want you to be stuck in superficial Christianity.

If I had to instruct a new believer or immature Christian, I would say the following. Put away your study Bible for now. Prayerfully read the word, starting with Romans, John, Colossians, Galatians, Titus, 1 and 2 Timothy, and Ephesians. Read these over and over, memorizing and meditating on passages where God speaks to you. Journal (or write) when you find a moving passage and write what God speaks to you. Get under a teacher that is focused on mentoring Christians into a deep fellowship with God. A teacher who doesn't feel threatened when people begin to wean off a dependence on being man taught, and begin learning how to be Spirit taught.

There is nothing wrong with being a babe in Christ. Immaturity is only the state we all must pass through before we become mature. It's only when we stay in infancy that there is a problem. A teacher that is a codependent is not maturing either. If someone needs to be depended upon, their identity is wrapped up in what gratifies the flesh. Our goal must be to teach others how to depend upon the Spirit, and resist the temptation of pride.

New believers or believers who have never been taught this way need guiding. Most people don't know they have been given all things. Few have any idea of the working of the Spirit in their lives, much less the reality of the mind of Christ being revealed to the inner man. Consider the words of Jesus in **John 6:45**

"It is written in the prophets, `And they shall all be taught by God.' Therefore everyone who has heard and learned from the Father comes to Me.

We live in this promise. You and I are taught by God. The Spirit is calling you to seek, so you can be taught what you need and what the body needs in order to mature in Christ. Each of us have this calling. When each person is receiving, each person plays a role in the church. Look at **1 Corinthians 14:29-32**

[29] Let two or three prophets speak, and let the others judge.
[30] But if *anything* is revealed to another who sits by, let the first keep silent.
[31] For you can all prophesy one by one, that all may learn and all may be encouraged.
[32] And the spirits of the prophets are subject to the prophets.

Not all are called to prophesy, so this isn't a warning that introverted people must speak before the church. As a reminder, the calling of a prophet is to make plain the hidden truths of God's word. The Spirit reveals something in the word to us, and we are called to share this with the church.

Those who are mature in the Spirit are called to both give place to God's revelation to others, and to judge (or evaluate) what is being revealed by comparing it to what has already been revealed through the prophets – which is the scriptures. The point of this is because God doesn't only use the pastor to edify the church. The Spirit reveals to each of us things that will edify (or grow) the church. Most churches have excluded this ministry of the Spirit, but we can still edify one another in informal settings. Or pastors can try to lead others back into a New Testament style worship gathering. Teaching and preaching are important ministries, but so is the call to let the Spirit flow among the congregation. Both need to remain unhindered.

There is never a time when we will learn all that God has in store for us. There is no reason for teachers to fear becoming unneeded. God does not reveal everything through one person, and we can always glean from teachers. But we must not make the pulpit a replacement for the Spirit's teaching to each believer.

Also, the more faithful we are in pointing people to Christ and teaching them to be Spirit led, the more God will reveal to us. As we are faithful, we are accounted as trustworthy. We are not better teachers by hoarding larger crowds, but by producing mature disciples.

As students of the word, we must live by the promise of God's revelation. The world tries to crowd our lives with entertainment, recreation, activities, work, and countless other distractions. We must make eternal things the highest priority.

The Apostle Peter said, "Seeing all these things shall be destroyed, what manner of men and women should you be in godly conduct?" This world is passing away. The TV shows that convince us they are too important to miss will be forgotten in a few months. Are they more worthy of our investment of time than what God has prepared for us to discover? Are hobbies a good trade off for God's eternal gifts of the Spirit?

Most of the things that fill up our lives are not sinful. The question is not sin or no-sin. The right question is, "What is the greatest investment for our lives? That which is passing away, or the things that can never pass?"

Live by the promise of **Jeremiah 33:3**

`Call to Me, and I will answer you, and show you great and mighty things, which you do not know.'

God delights in revealing His secret treasures to you. The Bible says, "Delight yourself in the Lord and He will give you the desires of your heart." God delights in you, and when you recognize the value of His relationship, you'll discover what it means to be delighted in Him. Then He will shape the desires of your heart into what has real value, and then God will grant you the promises He has in store for you.

God is delighted when you learn to trust in His love, and learn to let yourself be loved by God. All the promises of the scripture are given as expressions of God's love for you. The mind of Christ is the fullness of God's revelation of His love, and the gifts of the Spirit to you.

Don't make study a duty. Set your life on a journey of discovery. Discover His love. Discover the storehouse He has prepared for you. Discover the fellowship of the Spirit. God has blessed you with the gift of revelation so you can know His mind, and discover the joy of the deeper life of fellowship. A fellowship that cannot be imagined by anyone who has not learned to trust God enough to seek. It's all yours. Search and you will find His treasures stored up for you. That is God's guarantee!

Discussion Questions

Read 2 Peter 1:20-21, John 14:26, and 2 Timothy 2:15. Is the revelation of God's truth limited to a special anointed class of Christians?

Is it possible to misinterpret scripture?

Does God give us revelation that only we can see?

Review 1 Corinthians 2:14-16. How do you know the difference between the Spirit's revelation and our own ideas and assumptions?

If we have the mind of Christ through the presence of the Holy Spirit, how do we draw from His mind?

Review 1 Corinthians 2:9-11. Is this speaking of what will be revealed in heaven, or does it apply to your life today?

If the Spirit searches the deep things of God and reveals them to us, why do many Christians struggle to grow in their understanding?

Reread verse 11. Explain what this means to the Christian.

Read John 6:45, Jeremiah 31:34, and Hebrews 8:11. What do these passages tell us about the New Covenant working of the Holy Spirit?

Read Proverbs 20:5 and John 7:38-39. How does this apply to your Christian life?

Review 1 Corinthians 14:29-32. How can this be applied in today's church?

Has God revealed anything to you in this chapter? If so, explain.

Renewing the Mind

You might be surprised at how much instruction the New Testament gives us on renewing our minds, yet this is neglected in most of our lives. When I fail to renew my mind, it's a guarantee that my mind will be drawn back into the flesh. Let's look at **Ephesians 4:22-24**

22 that you put off, concerning your former conduct, the old man which grows corrupt according to the deceitful lusts,

23 and be renewed in the spirit of your mind,

24 and that you put on the new man which was created according to God, in true righteousness and holiness.

Renewal is not works. We are putting on the new man, which God created and gave us. This is referring to the lifestyle of the Spirit. The old nature is dead and buried with Christ. Your new life is what was raised with Christ. Even so, there must be a conscious effort to put off the former conduct of the old man, so we are not drawn back into a fleshly way of thinking.

Our minds can't operate in a vacuum. When we decide to stop doing something without bringing something better in, we are creating a void. That void will be filled. If there is no renewal, we'll fill that space with other fleshly ways of thinking, which will emerge in our conduct, or our mind will return to what we are trying to remove.

The command is to put off and put on. We put on the conduct of our new man by renewing our minds in the type of spiritual thinking that allows our inner man to thrive. It is a call to be renewed in the Spirit through our mind. The Bible says that the mind set on the flesh produces death, but the mind on the Spirit produces life and peace.[37]

You are not trying to become holy. The above scripture clearly explains that your new spirit was created in true righteousness and

---

[37] Romans 8:6

holiness. You aren't trying to become righteous. You are teaching your mind how to experience in the soul what is already a reality in the Spirit.

You aren't becoming. You are renewing.

We live in a fallen world. In our daily life in this world, we are picking up the dust. Dust on our feet does not change who we are. But it does affect us. Dirt is washed away. This is one of the roles of the Holy Spirit in our lives. Look at **Titus 3:5-6**

> [5] not by works of righteousness which we have done, but according to His mercy He saved us, through the washing of regeneration and renewing of the Holy Spirit,
> [6] whom He poured out on us abundantly through Jesus Christ our Savior,

Our salvation was taken care of when we turned to Christ to trust in His completed work. We received the washing of the Spirit when we were regenerated, which is our new birth in Christ. Then we are renewed through the Spirit as a daily process. You are regenerated once, but renewed continuously. Regeneration means to be recreated or to be given new life. To renew means to be made new. It's to take something and bring it back to its original condition. You can only be given life one time, for once you are alive, there is no need to give your spirit life. But renewal is daily. Look at **2 Corinthians 4:16**

> Therefore we do not lose heart. Even though our outward man is perishing, yet the inward *man* is being renewed day by day.

Your inner man is a partaker of God's own nature,[38] and has the life of the Spirit. Your inner man has eternal life, but your outer man is temporal. You must take the daily renewal of the Spirit and make it part of the life that is still bound to this world.

Jesus gave an illustration of this truth in John 13. Jesus took water and a basin and began washing the disciple's feet. It was a lesson in service and humility, but tucked into this event is another important lesson.

---

[38] 2 Peter 1:4

When Jesus came to Peter, he refused to allow him to wash his feet. When He warned that unless he humbled himself, he could have no part with Christ, Peter went to the opposite extreme. "Not my feet only, but also my hands and head." Now let's look at Jesus' teaching in **John 13:10-11**

> ¹⁰ Jesus said to him, "He who is bathed needs only to wash *his* feet, but is completely clean; and you are clean, but not all of you."
>
> ¹¹ For He knew who would betray Him; therefore He said, "You are not all clean."

Judas wasn't clean because he never trusted in Christ. We see from several tidbits in the four gospels, that Judas was a thief from the beginning. He looked at Jesus as a means of gain in this world. He followed as long as he thought Jesus was going to become the earthly king of Israel, but once Jesus began to foretell of the cross and His death, Judas began falling away. He then sought for an opportunity to make money on the way out, so he betrayed Jesus for thirty pieces of silver. In that era, that's the equivalent of five or seeks weeks of pay.

But to those who were of faith, Jesus teaches an important lesson. Later that same night, Jesus teaches that they are already clean because of the word He has spoken to them.[39] The church is also told they are cleansed by the washing of the water by the word.[40] The word is Christ, and we are made clean through Christ. This is explained in **John 1:1-3, 14**

> ¹ In the beginning was the Word, and the Word was with God, and the Word was God.
>
> ² He was in the beginning with God.
>
> ³ All things were made through Him, and without Him nothing was made that was made.
>
> ...
>
> ¹⁴ And the Word became flesh and dwelt among us, and we

---

[39] John 15:3
[40] Ephesians 5:26

beheld His glory, the glory as of the only begotten of the Father, full of grace and truth.

The word of God is God, and Jesus is the word made flesh. This is why the Bible teaches that we are cleansed of our sins through Christ, and that we are washed clean through the word. Then we are renewed back to our right appearance daily as we are washed in the word through the Spirit of our minds.

When Peter requested a complete rewashing, he was denied. "He that has been bathed only needs to wash his feet. Everything else is clean."

The average Christian is like Peter. When we get some filth from this world, we think we are now unclean. We beg God for reforgiveness, ask to be rewashed and made clean, but the Spirit gives us the same answer as Jesus gave Peter. You are already bathed by the washing of regeneration. You only need renewal – washing your feet.

Only that which is coming in contact with the dust of this world needs to be washed. Everything else is clean. Your life is clean if you are in Christ. Only the part of your life that encounters the world needs to be renewed. In this case, the feet needing to be washed is symbolic of our minds. The world can only enter our lives through the mind, but if the mind is being renewed daily, no filth can accumulate. The purpose of washing is so we don't get so used to filth that we accept it as part of our life. Look at **Romans 12:2**

And do not be conformed to this world, but be transformed by the renewing of your mind, that you may prove what *is* that good and acceptable and perfect will of God.

The word 'prove' in this passage is the Greek word, 'dokimazo', which means: to test or prove something by examining it to see if it is genuine. Do you struggle to discern God's will? If so, the problem is not trying to find God's will, but transforming our minds out of the world so we can clearly see God's will.

If you stomped around in mud, would you willingly track it into your house? Would it prevent you from putting on your good shoes and going out? Would it be a distraction from other things? Most of us would want to clean our feet before putting on clean socks. If we put good shoes over our filthy feet, it would be a distraction and uncomfortable.

In the same sense, the filth of this world creates a consistent distraction. How can you pursue the things of the Spirit if you feel the cares of this life clinging to you? Yet as you consistently renew your mind in the word, spiritual clarity is the natural outcome. You'll begin to stop focusing on the cares of this life, and the will of God will be proven in your heart. There has to be a daily renewal. Let's also bring in **Colossians 3:9-10**

9 Do not lie to one another, since you have put off the old man with his deeds,

10 and have put on the new *man* who is renewed in knowledge according to the image of Him who created him,

Notice, you have put off the old man, yet as we saw earlier, we must daily put off the deeds of the old man. The flesh still desires the old way. Jesus illustrated this in **Luke 5:37-39**

37 "And no one puts new wine into old wineskins; or else the new wine will burst the wineskins and be spilled, and the wineskins will be ruined.

38 "But new wine must be put into new wineskins, and both are preserved.

39 "And no one, having drunk old *wine*, immediately desires new; for he says, `The old is better.'"

Some translations use the word 'bottle', but in the ancient world, wine was stored in airtight wineskins. When juiced grapes finish fermenting, it is stored, but must be stored in a new skin. There is still yeast activity going on, and carbon dioxide is the byproduct. As this gas continues to be emitted, the skins begin to stretch. An old skin is no longer flexible, and cannot stretch, so when the pressure builds, it bursts.

The new wine is a symbol of the Holy Spirit. The Spirit cannot enter into the life of the old man. The old nature is not capable of receiving it, but our new life can. We can receive the Spirit, and we can expand to receive what the Spirit is producing within us.

Even to those who have received the new life, Jesus says, "No one having drunk the old wine immediately desires the new, for he says, 'The old is better.'" This is the new believer.

When someone first comes to Christ, they still have the mindset that the old is better. It isn't until we begin experiencing the new wine that we mature in our taste. A new Christian still has many worldly habits, but as they grow, they begin losing their taste for the old, and begin desiring the new wine of the Spirit.

This is likely true in your life, for we all have varying desires of the old life we were taken out of. We easily recognize the value of leaving our dead nature behind, but the flesh still desires the old wine. Losing our desire for the old wine is not always immediate.

As we renew our minds, we become receivers of the new wine, and learn to enjoy the new life over the old. But that doesn't happen until we start experiencing the new life of the Spirit.

When I don't see what I have, the grass on the other side always looks greener. There must be knowledge of the new life first. That is part of renewing. As we read a moment ago, the new man is renewed through the knowledge of Christ. As we discover the depths of Christ and the treasures we have been given in the Spirit, the old wine begins to look worthless. The old way is indeed worthless, but cheap wine seems good to those who have never tasted the wine of the Spirit.

This is a daily lifestyle. If we famish our spiritual life, our soul will become weak spiritually, and a starving soul will crave anything set before it. Now let's look at **2 Corinthians 4:16**

Therefore we do not lose heart. Even though our outward man is perishing, yet the inward *man* is being renewed day by day.

Our tendency is to gorge and fast. We load up on Sunday and then fast until Wednesday. We study when something moves us, then neglect our daily renewal.

What would happen to our bodies if we made a habit of feasting for a day and then starving the other six days? Our bodies would be unregulated and unhealthy. Then we would gladly eat any food set before us, good or unhealthy.

Without a balanced diet and a consistent eating habit, we are limiting our health. It's no different with our spirit. If we don't daily feed and renew, we are limiting our spiritual health. Then we wonder why the flesh is stronger than our spiritual lives.

A mind starved of the Spirit will devour the things of the flesh. Lust, anger, worry, bitterness, and all the anxieties of this life will appear to be treasures to the fleshly mind. But God has provided a system of renewal. One of God's great promises is freely given to us in **Philippians 4:6-8**

> 6 Be anxious for nothing, but in everything by prayer and supplication, with thanksgiving, let your requests be made known to God;
> 7 and the peace of God, which surpasses all understanding, will guard your hearts and minds through Christ Jesus.
> 8 Finally, brethren, whatever things are true, whatever things *are* noble, whatever things *are* just, whatever things *are* pure, whatever things *are* lovely, whatever things *are* of good report, if *there is* any virtue and if *there is* anything praiseworthy-- meditate on these things.

Notice, God does not merely tell us to reject anxiety. He calls for us to put it off while putting on the good things. The mind isn't left in a vacuum. We are taking the negative thoughts away by setting our minds on the things of the Spirit.

If you've programmed your mind to dwell on the negative, this is not an easy process. But remember, you are not trying to climb the hill of impossibility. God has placed you at the top of the hill and now calls for you to not allow yourself to be drawn back into fleshly ways of thinking.

When thoughts arise that create anxiety, God calls for you to take your mind off those thoughts by focusing on the good things He provides. Sometimes we accomplish this by memorizing scripture. We can set our minds on good by praying, singing, reading faith-affirming books or articles, or listening to faith-affirming teachings.

If we do these things, God has promised that He will guard our hearts and minds and give us the peace that goes beyond human comprehension.

We reject negativism as an act of faith. We set our minds on God's goodness as an act of faith. My flesh looks at what I don't like and calls for me to grumble and brood. The Spirit calls for me to roll my cares onto God's shoulders, and trust His promise that He works all things for my good. Then I can focus on the fruit of the Spirit, knowing that God has taken away the burdens of the flesh.

When our spirit is healthy and thriving, our spiritual life drives out the ways of the flesh. The flesh only has strength when the mind is famished of the spirit.

If I trust in my flesh and depend on the world to provide good circumstances, then I will live in frustration and disappointment. I am also rejecting God's call and stepping outside of His promises. I cannot claim God's peace while grumbling and complaining. I can't ask God to guard my heart while I am giving it to the world.

There is another important part of the Spirit's renewal that most people don't understand because of how many misinterpret an important scripture. Look at **John 16:7-11**

7 "Nevertheless I tell you the truth. It is to your advantage that I go away; for if I do not go away, the Helper will not come to you; but if I depart, I will send Him to you.

8 "And when He has come, He will convict the world of sin, and of righteousness, and of judgment:

9 "of sin, because they do not believe in Me;

10 "of righteousness, because I go to My Father and you see Me no more;

11 "of judgment, because the ruler of this world is judged.

Jesus doesn't leave us in doubt as to His meaning, because He interprets His words for us. But most teachings on this scripture reinterpret contrary to what Jesus said. Most people teach that the Holy Spirit convicts the believer of sin, but Jesus does not say this.

Sin has been destroyed for those who are in Christ, and the Bible says it has been taken out of the way. This is explained in detail in the first book of this series, so I won't go into this here. But we will dig into the above scripture.

The main point of this teaching is so we know the Spirit is our helper. He helps us fulfill the great commission by convicting the world of sin. This helps the world to recognize the gift of forgiveness and eternal life by stripping away self-glorification and false man-made righteousness.

He convicts us of righteousness, and reveals that the ruler of this world (Satan) has been judged. Has been. This agrees with Colossians 2:15, where we are told Jesus disarmed principalities and triumphed over them on the cross.

This gives us complete confidence. We need not fear Satan, for he has been defeated. We don't carry the burden of convicting people of sin, for the Spirit convicts and draws people to Christ[41] where they can be saved. We need not worry about our sins, for the Spirit continues to unveil our gift of righteousness to us.

Only one of these roles applies to the Christian. 'Of sin,' is to the world because "They do not believe in Me." This cannot be the conviction of sin for the Christian, for we DO believe in Christ. The Spirit's judgment is also not to the Christian, for we are not the ones defeated. We are not the rulers of this world. We are the ones in God's righteousness.

And this is the role of renewal we should understand. When you sin, the Spirit is constantly revealing your righteousness to you. It was never righteousness by human effort. Righteousness is a gift. You are the righteousness of God in Christ. You don't create righteousness; your righteousness is the same as God's.

Most people falsely teach that we are convicted of sin, but the truth is that we are convicted of righteousness. To convict is to try someone and find them guilty. To convict the world of sin is an accurate statement. They are guilty and are under condemnation.

---

[41] John 6:44

Renewing the Mind

To convict is to try someone according to the law and find them guilty. That person is now a convict. They will remain under condemnation until they turn to Christ. Anyone in Christ has the promise of Romans 8:1, there is now no condemnation to those who are in Christ Jesus. We are in the Spirit (See Romans 8:9) and cannot be condemned again.

To convict us of righteousness is a powerful statement. To be declared guilty of righteousness is not a word of condemnation, but a declaration that we have been tried and found righteous because we do believe in Christ.

To help understand this, let's visit a controversy that occurred at the birth of the New Covenant church. Salvation began at the house of Israel. The scriptures were given through the Jews, and all the apostles were Jews.

In the Old Covenant, in order for a Gentile (or non-Jew) to enter into God's covenant, they had to become a proselyte. This means they learned the customs and laws of the Old Covenant and converted to Judaism.

This mindset remained in the early church. The Jewish Christians still thought salvation was a call to become a Jew AND to trust in Christ. God dispelled that notion when He gave Peter a vision of a dinner invitation filled with animals that were unclean according to the law. These were the animals the Old Testament forbade the Jews to eat because they were unclean. God commanded, "Arise Peter, kill and eat."

Peter refused by saying, "I have never eaten anything unclean."

God rebuked Peter by saying, "What the Lord has cleansed, don't you call 'unclean'." When the vision ended, two men were knocking at the door, asking for Peter. Cornelius had been instructed by an angel to call for Peter to hear the gospel. God then commanded Peter to go with these men, asking no questions.

God put Peter in a position where he was forced to break the Old Covenant laws by housing with Gentiles and dining with them. The Lord was dismantling Peter's mindset of the Old Covenant because it was fulfilled in Christ and done away with.[42]

---

[42] 2 Corinthians 3:7-11, 1 Corinthians 13:10, Hebrews 10:1-10

When Peter preached to this house filled with curious Gentiles, they believed the gospel, and the Holy Spirit fell on them, and used many signs to prove to Peter that the gift of God was not to Jews, but to all. This didn't end the controversy. Paul was called to be the apostle to the Gentiles, but as new churches were born, Jewish Christians began going to those churches and teaching them that they had to submit to the Old Covenant Law of Moses in order to finish the work of salvation.

This created a major dispute between the missionaries to the Gentiles (including Paul) and the Christians who were coming out of a legalistic mindset. The dispute became so pervasive, the apostles called a church counsel to discuss the matter. With that background, let's pick up the discussion in **Acts 15:7-11**

> 7 And when there had been much dispute, Peter rose up *and* said to them: "Men *and* brethren, you know that a good while ago God chose among us, that by my mouth the Gentiles should hear the word of the gospel and believe.
> 8 "So God, who knows the heart, acknowledged them by giving them the Holy Spirit, just as *He did* to us,
> 9 "and made no distinction between us and them, purifying their hearts by faith.
> 10 "Now therefore, why do you test God by putting a yoke on the neck of the disciples which neither our fathers nor we were able to bear?
> 11 "But we believe that through the grace of the Lord Jesus Christ we shall be saved in the same manner as they."

There are two things I want you to see in this passage. God made no distinction between the Jews who were under the law and the Gentiles who were outside of the Old Testament law. He purified their hearts by faith.

Faith in Christ is the ONLY requirement God has put on any believer. You are purified by faith. When you believe, God accounts you as righteous, which means He credits you with His own righteousness. The Bible says, "You are the righteousness of God in

Christ."[43] This is why Jesus can say, "You are already clean because of the word I have spoken to you." You hear the word, which is the gospel of grace through Christ, and when you believe, you are cleansed by the power of the Holy Spirit.

There is no such thing as partial cleansing. It is not a partnership where if we do our part of keeping the law, God will reward us by doing His part. Our only role is faith. God reveals through faith, and calls us to believe in what He has revealed. When we believe, we are made clean. Once the Spirit cleanses us, that is the completed work of God. Period. What God has cleansed, no man can call unclean.

The second thing to note is the declaration that the yoke of the law was a burden that the Jews of that day couldn't bear, nor could their fathers bear. No one disputed this truth. Even Jesus said this when He told the Jewish leaders, "None of you keeps the law."[44] They wanted to condemn Jesus to death, but none of them disputed the truth that they were not keeping the law. They did their best, but according to the Bible, even one offense makes you guilty of the whole law.[45]

The main part of the dispute was the law's demand that a person be circumcised. Though circumcision was the focus at that moment, the heart of the problem was going back to the law. To go back to a system which was designed to be a foreshadow of Christ, would now be a denial of Christ.

The apostles spoke of the unbearable yoke of the law. The yoke of the law was not circumcision, for this procedure was done shortly after birth. Once completed, it was in the past. The purpose of their opposition was that circumcision was the demand to put the Gentiles under the law. Then they would be under the yoke of burden, which is trying to keep the law. The same law that neither the apostles, nor their forefathers could bear. Why put the Christian under a system which was done away with in Christ?[46] Yet

---

43 2 Corinthians 5:21
44 John 7:19
45 James 2:10, Galatians 5:3
46 Hebrews 8:13

the Judaizers (Jewish Christians teaching the law), were trying to put on the Gentile Christians a legal system that was impossible to fulfill.

Christ redeemed us out of the law, but as Galatians says, "You who desire to be under the law have fallen from grace." This is a critical truth. Look at **Romans 6:14**

For sin shall not have dominion over you, for you are not under law but under grace.

Now this is an important truth for renewal, but to grasp the bigger picture, we need to bring in **1 Corinthians 15:56-57**

[56] The sting of death *is* sin, and the strength of sin *is* the law.

[57] But thanks *be* to God, who gives us the victory through our Lord Jesus Christ.

Here is the vital truth and how it applies to the Spirit's conviction of righteousness. The strength of sin is the law. Anyone under the law is empowering sin. But sin cannot have dominion over the believer, because we are not under the law but under grace.

Since this is true, the Spirit renews us by continuously disarming sin by convicting us of righteousness. As we are affirmed in God's righteousness by grace, we are made to understand that sin cannot have dominion over us. When sin is disarmed, we are set free. When the law is preached, sin is given the strength to enslave.

Judiazers are still in the church today, teaching a modern day form of the law. It may not demand circumcision, but it does demand that we submit to the law. The Bible warns that anyone who submits to the law is indebted to keep the whole law, and since the strength of sin is the law, we are giving sin dominion over us. A dominion that can only exist when we enter disbelief in grace by trusting in the law. Law-trusters do not believe that Christ's work is completed, so they must re-enter the flesh to keep the law. Focusing on the law is a work of the flesh, though it is called spiritual by many.

But the Spirit is constantly convicting us of righteousness and unveiling the work of Christ. When we sin (and when we don't sin), the Spirit is declaring our righteousness, so we learn to trust in the power of the Spirit and not in the weakness of the law.[47]

As we learn to have faith in God's righteousness, sin is weakened and we live in the promise, "Sin cannot have dominion over you." This promise is not to those who are under the law. This promise is only under grace. Under grace, righteousness reigns. Under the law, sin reigns. Look at **Romans 7:8**

> But sin, taking opportunity by the commandment, produced in me all *manner of evil* desire. For apart from the law sin *was* dead.

Stop and meditate on this vital truth. Apart from the law, sin was dead. The Christian is not under the law, but under grace.[48] Because you are not under the law, sin is dead. And how do you revive sin in your life? Let's continue in **Romans 7:9-11**

> [9] I was alive once without the law, but when the commandment came, sin revived and I died.
> [10] And the commandment, which *was* to *bring* life, I found to *bring* death.
> [11] For sin, taking occasion by the commandment, deceived me, and by it killed *me*.

Do you want to revive sin? Without the law, you live. When the law enters, the law gives life to sin and sin uses the commandment to slay anyone who fails in any point. This is why Christians are defeated. In Christ, they are made alive. But because the church exalts sin and reintroduces the law, those who once had life are persuaded to submit back under a form of religion that is dependent upon man's righteousness instead of God's. Then sin revives and defeats those who have been deceived into returning to a legalistic shadow of faith.

---

[47] Romans 8:3
[48] Romans 6:14

What is the answer? To the Galatian church the Bible laments, "You have fallen from grace and have become estranged from Christ because you have returned to the law,"[49] the Bible then gives the remedy. Look at **Galatians 5:18**

But if you are led by the Spirit, you are not under the law.

Return to faith in Christ and live by the Spirit. Stop looking at yourself. Stop looking at the law. Stop looking at sin. Stop exalting sin over the work of Christ. Look to Christ, receive the word, and allow the hearing of faith to again cause you to receive the miracle working power of the Spirit.[50]

The natural mind cannot receive the things of the Spirit, for they are foolishness to him.[51] The natural mind does not have faith in the power of God's grace. Human reasoning believes that if we turn our eyes from the law, this will empower sin, though God says the opposite. The natural mind does not grasp what is only understood in the Spirit, because grace can only be received through faith.

This is another reason why renewing is critical. Faith comes by hearing the word of God.[52] When the word is accurately taught, it will affirm faith in the Spirit, faith in God's promises, faith in Jesus' triumph over sin, and faith that grace can do what God promises. According to Titus 2:11-15, grace brings salvation to us, teaches us how to deny ungodliness and worldly lusts. Grace also teaches us how to live soberly, righteously, and godly in this present world. Grace also produces a people zealous for good works. Then to top it off, the Bible says that we should not be discouraged when people despise us, who trust in God's promise of grace.

Find anywhere that the law produces these things? According to the Bible, the law makes us guilty and no one doing the deeds of the law can be justified.[53] We've already seen that the law gives

---

[49] Galatians 5:4
[50] Galatians 3:5-7
[51] 1 Corinthians 2:14
[52] Romans 10:17
[53] Romans 3:19-20

Renewing the Mind

strength to sin, but the purpose of this is to create the knowledge of sin to the unbeliever.[54] To the Christian, we are renewed in the knowledge of Christ – not the knowledge of sin.

The role of the law is to convict the world of sin, and the Holy Spirit can use the law as it unveils the sinful condition of the unbeliever. But to the believer, the Spirit disarms sin. The believer is continuously convicted of righteousness, so we understand that we are free from sin and the law. The more we believe God's word, the more sin's power is stripped away.

Renew your mind. Rightly divide the word of truth, and supplement your spiritual nourishment by listening or reading from teachers who teach faith in God's promises. Do not allow yourself to be put back under the burden of the law, for there is no power for the believer in anything other than faith in the completed work of Christ.

We receive His power through faith. The completed work of Christ is received by faith, so the same power that raised Christ from the dead will give life to our mortal bodies. The working of the Spirit will begin emerging as fruit in our daily lives as we walk by faith. This is not promised to those who receive the law or believe in the power of sin.

Be renewed in the spirit of your mind, and roll the burdens of this life (including sin) onto God's shoulders where they belong. Let God worry about sin. You focus on the righteousness of God in Christ. Renew yourself in Christ and watch the weakness of the flesh become irrelevant!

---

[54] Romans 3:20

Discussion Questions

What does the Bible mean, "Be renewed in the Spirit of your mind?"

How is this different from the regeneration of the Holy Spirit?

Jesus taught that the disciples were already clean. How does His washing of feet, but refusal to completely rewash the disciples, apply to our lives?

Review Romans 12:2. How do we discover God's will for our lives?

Is it normal for a new Christian to have desires from the old life before Christ? How and why do our desires change?

Review John 16:7-11. Explain how Jesus interprets the role of the Spirit.

How is this different from the way this is commonly taught?

What does it mean to be convicted of righteousness?

Review Romans 6:14. How does grace defeat sin?

Read 2 Peter 1:3, Colossians 3:10, 1 Corinthians 15:56-57, and Romans 7:8-11. Do we renew our minds by studying the law? Or by the knowledge of Christ and His work given to us?

How does gaining the knowledge of Christ renew our minds?

Does guilt renew us?

Does faith in the righteousness of God given to us renew us?

Should we be teaching believers to look at their sins, or to look at the Bible's declaration that we are the righteousness of God in Christ? Which is of faith?

What is the Holy Spirit?

If you were raised in a traditional Christian environment, this may not be a question for you. However, this is still an important chapter, since there are many misconceptions of the Spirit in religious circles. Some claim the Spirit is a force that we tap into. Some claim that the Holy Spirit is an impersonal agent God uses to institute His will. In this section, we'll look at how the Bible describes the Holy Spirit, so we can have a deeper understanding of God.

The Spirit is mentioned 316 times in the New Testament. To put this into perspective, grace is mentioned 119 times. Salvation is mentioned 42 times. Sin is mentioned 110 times. Judgment is mentioned 68 times. But hell is only mentioned 13 times. In the King James version where the word for grave (Hades) and hell (Gehenna) are combined, that number is still only 23 times.

Since the Spirit is one of the most common subjects in the New Testament, just behind Jesus (935 times) and God (1188 times), this should tell us that the Bible places a lot of emphasis on the Spirit. Even so, unless you are in a Charismatic style church, the Spirit is rarely mentioned.

Let's first put to rest the idea of the Holy Spirit being an impersonal force. The Spirit directly spoke to the prophets to write the scriptures. When the apostles were seeking to replace Judas, the Bible says the following in **Acts 1:16-17**

16 "Men *and* brethren, this Scripture had to be fulfilled, which the Holy Spirit spoke before by the mouth of David concerning Judas, who became a guide to those who arrested Jesus;
17 "for he was numbered with us and obtained a part in this ministry."

The Spirit spoke to the prophets. He also spoke direct revelation during the time when Acts was being written. Look at **Acts 8:29**

Then the Spirit said to Philip, "Go near and overtake this chariot."

The Spirit's instruction directed Philip to share Christ with a man leaving Jerusalem and heading back to his homeland. When God was about to unveil the truth that Jesus' work was not only to the Jews, but also to the Gentiles, the Bible says in **Acts 10:19**

While Peter thought about the vision, the Spirit said to him, "Behold, three men are seeking you."

When Peter was confronted for breaking the Jewish law by eating and lodging with Gentiles, he starts his testimony in **Acts 11:12**

"Then the Spirit told me to go with them, doubting nothing. Moreover these six brethren accompanied me, and we entered the man's house."

When God called Saul, who was later renamed to Paul, **Acts 13:2** explains:

As they ministered to the Lord and fasted, the Holy Spirit said, "Now separate to Me Barnabas and Saul for the work to which I have called them."

An impersonal force does not speak. Part of the reason the Spirit is out of the minds of most Christians is because His role is to point to Christ and not Himself. Look at **John 16:13**

However, when He, the Spirit of truth, has come, He will guide you into all truth; for He will not speak on His own *authority*, but whatever He hears He will speak; and He will tell you things to come.

The Spirit of truth is the Holy Spirit. In John 16, Jesus calls the Spirit the Holy Spirit, Helper (or Comforter in KJV), and Spirit of Truth. The above statement about the Spirit is nearly identical to what Jesus says about Himself in John 8:28. Jesus says that He does not speak of Himself, but what He hears and sees from the Father.[55] When Jesus was the witness on earth, His testimony was to only speak what was heard from the Father. Once the Spirit became God's witness on earth, the Spirit does not speak of Himself, but testifies of Christ. Look at **John 15:26**

> But when the Helper comes, whom I shall send to you from the Father, the Spirit of truth who proceeds from the Father, He will testify of Me.

This also agrees with **1 John 5:7-8**
> [7] For there are three that bear witness in heaven: the Father, the Word, and the Holy Spirit; and these three are one.
> [8] And there are three that bear witness on earth: the Spirit, the water, and the blood; and these three agree as one.

During Jesus' earthly ministry, He said that He bears witness of the truth.[56] Then He explained to His disciples that it was necessary for Him to return to the Father, or else the Spirit cannot come.[57] Now the Spirit is among us, and He bears witness on the earth.

Jesus is God. The Spirit is God. The Father is God. To see this clearly, let's bring in a few passages. Let's start with the Holy Spirit. First look at **John 4:24**
> God *is* Spirit, and those who worship Him must worship in spirit and truth.

Add to this **2 Corinthians 3:17**
> Now the Lord is the Spirit; and where the Spirit of the Lord *is*, there *is* liberty.

The Lord is the Spirit. Yet, the Bible also says that Jesus is the Lord. The Bible compares the first man, Adam to Jesus, who is called the second Adam. Jesus called Himself 'The Son of Man', referring to His human role of reversing the curse of the first man,

---

[55] John 15:15
[56] John 18:37
[57] John 16:7

Adam. In the midst of this explanation, the Bible says in **1 Corinthians 15:47**

> The first man *was* of the earth, *made* of dust; the second Man *is* the Lord from heaven.

Jesus is called 'The Lord from heaven.' Then the Father is called the Lord. Look at **Matthew 11:25**

> At that time Jesus answered and said, "I thank You, Father, Lord of heaven and earth, that You have hidden these things from *the* wise and prudent and have revealed them to babes."

The Bible calls Jesus the creator, the Spirit the creator, and the Father the creator. This is a little less clear with the Father, since the creation account does not refer to God as Father. This wasn't revealed to us until the Son was born. Yet, it is still seen if we have eyes to look for it. First look at **Genesis 1:26-27**

> 26 Then God said, "Let Us make man in Our image, according to Our likeness; let them have dominion over the fish of the sea, over the birds of the air, and over the cattle, over all the earth and over every creeping thing that creeps on the earth."
> 27 So God created man in His *own* image; in the image of God He created him; male and female He created them.

Who is the 'Us'? God is not talking to angels, for they have no power to create. Not once do we see an angel taking part in creation. Not once do we see anything but God being credited with creation. The 'Us' is the Father, Son, and Spirit. Now look at the beginning of creation in **Genesis 1:1-3**

> 1 In the beginning God created the heavens and the earth.
> 2 The earth was without form, and void; and darkness *was* on the face of the deep. And the Spirit of God was hovering over the face of the waters.
> 3 Then God said, "Let there be light"; and there was light.

God created the heavens and the earth, but then credit is given to the Spirit of God. Then the Bible gives credit to the Son. Look at **John 1:1-3**

¹ In the beginning was the Word, and the Word was with God, and the Word was God.

² He was in the beginning with God.

³ All things were made through Him, and without Him nothing was made that was made.

Jesus is the Word and the Word is God. All things were made by Him, Jesus. Seven verses later, the Bible reaffirms this by saying that Jesus came into the world He made, but was rejected. This is affirmed again in **Colossians 1:14-17**

¹⁴ in whom we have redemption through His blood, the forgiveness of sins.

¹⁵ He is the image of the invisible God, the firstborn over all creation.

¹⁶ For by Him all things were created that are in heaven and that are on earth, visible and invisible, whether thrones or dominions or principalities or powers. All things were created through Him and for Him.

¹⁷ And He is before all things, and in Him all things consist.

Not only did Jesus create all things in both heaven and earth, but in Christ dwells the fullness of the Godhead. The truth is that you can't separate God. God reveals Himself through the Son, Spirit, and Father, but these are not three Gods, but one. This is not merely a New Testament revelation. Look in the Old Testament book of **Isaiah 48:16-17**

¹⁶ "Come near to Me, hear this: I have not spoken in secret from the beginning; From the time that it was, I *was* there. And now the Lord GOD and His Spirit Have sent Me."

¹⁷ Thus says the LORD, your Redeemer, The Holy One of Israel: "I *am* the LORD your God, Who teaches you to profit, Who leads you by the way you should go.

The Lord God and His Spirit have sent Me. Who is the 'me' speaking? The next verse explains, our Redeemer. This is God's foretelling of Jesus the Redeemer who would first come to Israel, the Jewish people, and then God goes on to explain that through His visitation, the Gentiles would also be saved.[58] To insure His people understand that the Redeemer, the Spirit, and the LORD are not separate deities, **Isaiah 44:6** explains:

> Thus says the LORD, the King of Israel, And his Redeemer, the LORD of hosts:`I *am* the First and I *am* the Last; Besides Me *there is* no God.

When you see LORD in all caps, it denotes that the word being translated is Jehovah, which is from the Hebrew word YHWH. Vowels were added to make it translatable. In this passage, the LORD is Jehovah, and His Redeemer is Jehovah. Yet, God declares that beside Him there is no other God.

Add to this that Jesus is called 'The First and the Last' in Revelation 1:11, 1:17, 2:8, 22:13.

Before we move on, I want to address the passage in Colossians we read earlier. It refers to Jesus as the firstborn over all creation. Some have attempted to use this to claim Jesus is a creation and not the creator. Some even argue that Jesus was created, and then created all other things. But the Bible says that God created ALL things.

The word 'firstborn' is a position of honor, not a claim of being created. It should be clear that Jesus being born does not negate His divine nature. This is clarified in **Isaiah 9:6**

> For unto us a Child is born, Unto us a Son is given; And the government will be upon His shoulder. And His name will be called Wonderful, Counselor, Mighty God, Everlasting Father, Prince of Peace.

Notice, the child is born, but the Son is given. And how can a created child be called 'Mighty God'? There is a comparison being made. Adam was the first man, and Jesus is called the second

---

[58] Isaiah 49:6, Isaiah 62:2, Isaiah 66:12, 19

What is the Holy Spirit?

Adam. Technically, Adam was first, but Jesus is given the honor of firstborn over Adam. The inheritance of the earth was stripped away from the first Adam, and given to the second Adam.

The Bible gives several examples that foreshadow this. Esau was the firstborn and by birthright, he was the heir to the lineage that would become Israel, which would lead to the Messiah, Jesus Christ. But God took the honor from Esau, and gave it to Jacob. Esau was of the flesh, but Jacob became the son of promise.

Another example was Ishmael and Isaac. Abraham was given the promise of a son through Sarah, but as the time kept passing, he and Sarah became impatient, and decided to father a son by marrying a servant girl. It was an act of the flesh, and though Ishmael was the firstborn son, Isaac was given the honor of firstborn and was called the son of promise.

Another example was the sons of Joseph. When Joseph's father was on his deathbed, he called Joseph to bring in his two sons. Traditionally, the right hand was placed on the firstborn son's head, so Joseph placed his children in the right place to be blessed. But Jacob crossed his hands and placed it on the younger son's head and blessed him as the firstborn. His name was Ephraim. Now look at God's declaration in **Jeremiah 31:9b**

For I am a Father to Israel, And Ephraim *is* My firstborn.

Jacob's name was changed to Israel, and his twelve sons became the twelve tribes of Israel. Ephraim was not even close to the firstborn position. Ephraim was actually the grandson of Jacob, but he claimed (or adopted) Ephraim and Manasseh as his own children and gave them an inheritance as sons. Ephraim was the youngest, but God called Ephraim His firstborn.

Firstborn is a declaration of a son's position in the inheritance, and God uses this as a picture of His work. Adam was of the flesh, but the second Adam is Jesus, Lord from Heaven. According to the flesh, Adam was the firstborn, but according to God's authority, Jesus was declared to be the firstborn over all creation.

Understanding the inseparable Godhead is important so we can understand the Spirit. The Spirit is called the Spirit of Christ, the

Spirit of God, and the Holy Spirit. Let's bring in another passage. Look also at **Romans 8:9**

> But you are not in the flesh but in the Spirit, if indeed the Spirit of God dwells in you. Now if anyone does not have the Spirit of Christ, he is not His.

The Spirit of Christ is the Spirit of God. The Spirit of God is the Holy Spirit. This is why Jesus can say the following in **John 14:23**

> Jesus answered and said to him, "If anyone loves Me, he will keep My word; and My Father will love him, and We will come to him and make Our home with him."

When you think of the Spirit, do not think of a lesser God. Don't try to split God into a neat theological package. People often ask if we should pray to the Father or pray to Jesus. Pray to God without worrying about methods and procedures. What is important is that we pray in Jesus' name. Listen to the words of Jesus in these two passages.

John 14:13-14

> [13] "And whatever you ask in My name, that I will do, that the Father may be glorified in the Son.
> [14] "If you ask anything in My name, I will do *it*.

John 16:26-27

> [26] "In that day you will ask in My name, and I do not say to you that I shall pray the Father for you;
> [27] "for the Father Himself loves you, because you have loved Me, and have believed that I came forth from God.

The important thing is that you pray in Christ name because you are trusting in the work He accomplished for you. You are believing that you have the right and privilege to come before the throne of grace with confidence. You aren't approaching God because you have made yourself worthy, but because you are trusting in Christ. And when your prayers fall short, you have the promise of help from our Comforter as explained in **Romans 8:26-27**

What is the Holy Spirit?

[26] Likewise the Spirit also helps in our weaknesses. For we do not know what we should pray for as we ought, but the Spirit Himself makes intercession for us with groanings which cannot be uttered.

[27] Now He who searches the hearts knows what the mind of the Spirit *is*, because He makes intercession for the saints according to *the will of* God.

Trust in the promise that the Spirit is the strength of the Christian life. The Spirit transforms us into Christ's image. The Spirit puts to death the deeds of the body and suppresses our tendency to sin. The Spirit intercedes for us when we don't know what or how to pray. The Spirit reveals to us the mind of Christ.

Our calling is to be filled with the Spirit. We do this by taking our eyes off our abilities, off our sins and weaknesses, off our religious efforts, and off our works. We put our focus on Christ, and trust in God's Spirit to bring us into the will of God. Let's begin wrapping this chapter up with **Romans 8:11**

But if the Spirit of Him who raised Jesus from the dead dwells in you, He who raised Christ from the dead will also give life to your mortal bodies through His Spirit who dwells in you.

Raising Jesus from the dead was the hard part. If the Spirit can accomplish this, and we have that same Spirit in us, then He also has the power to overcome the weakness of the flesh with the life and power of the Spirit. Trust in the promise of the Spirit. You have the promise, and all things are yours by promise. Those who trust become receivers.

I know this chapter has thrown a lot of verses at the reader, but it's important to see that these are not a few verses taken out of context. The scriptures are painting a robust picture of the power of the Spirit's work in our lives. God did not save us and then leave us to fend for ourselves. We have the indwelling of the Spirit and all the promises that are through the Spirit.

Your weaknesses are not a limitation because the Christian life does not rest on your shoulders. You are joined to Christ, and the

Spirit guarantees the success of those who learn to walk by faith. Not faith in our performance, but faith in the power of God.

Discussion Questions

Why do you think that the Spirit could not come to be the witness on earth until the Son returned to the Father?

If the Spirit speaks, directs, teaches, comforts, and transforms us into Christ's image, why do many think of the Spirit as an impersonal force?

Review Genesis 1:26-27. Why did God say, "Let Us make man in Our image," but then the Bible says that God created man in His own image - with no reference to anything but God alone?

Read Genesis 1:1, John 1:1-4, and John 1:10-11. Why does the Bible say that God created the earth, but then says the world was made through Christ?

Review Isaiah 48:16-17. How can the Lord and His Spirit send the Lord our Redeemer?

Review Isaiah 44:6. How can the Lord and His Redeemer, the Lord, say I (not we) am the first and the last, beside Me there is no God?

Read 1 Corinthians 3:15, 1 Corinthians 6:19, and John 14:23. How does Jesus and the Father make their home within us?

Review Romans 8:26-27. How does this help you rest in faith when your prayers seem inadequate?

Review Romans 8:11. How does this apply to your daily Christian life?

Read Romans 8:2. What definition is given to the Spirit, and what role does He play in our lives?

Read Romans 8:15. What does the Spirit reveal to us?

Read 2 Corinthians 3:17-18. What role does the Spirit have for our life in this passage?

Read Galatians 4:6. Whose name is given to the Spirit and what is His role here?

Read Romans 8:9. Why does the Bible call the Holy Spirit the Spirit of God, and then the Spirit of Christ?

Read 1 Corinthians 12:13 and Ephesians 4:4-7. Is the Holy Spirit, Spirit of Christ, the Spirit of God, and the Spirit of the Father separate spirits, or different perspectives of one God?

Do any of these passages challenge the way you have been taught about the Holy Spirit?

What is the Holy Spirit?

Be Filled with the Spirit

You have an amazing gift. The Old Testament saints could never be indwelled by the Spirit, but the Christian is the temple of the Spirit. The Old Testament saints had to travel to the temple to encounter God. Today, where you go is the temple of the Holy Spirit.

The church building is NOT the house of God; you are. The church is where God's people gather. When two or three temples (believers) are gathered together, they are the church and are the body of Christ.[59] We may gather in a building, but the building is nothing but an empty shell. It is not where God dwells. You are where God dwells. This is something the Old Testament saints foretold in the scriptures by God's revelation, but could not experience.

When you see the Holy Spirit in the Old Testament, He comes upon men. The Bible uses phrases like, "The Spirit of the Lord came upon him," but it did not inhabit men and women. Not understanding this leads to misconceptions. For example, look at **Psalm 51:10-11**

[10] Create in me a clean heart, O God, And renew a steadfast spirit within me.

[11] Do not cast me away from Your presence, And do not take Your Holy Spirit from me.

Verse 11 isn't possible in the New Testament. The Old Testament believers had to measure up to the law or risk losing favor. Every person lost favor in the Old Covenant, for no one succeeded in measuring up to the law. Even David, who wrote the Psalm above, fell several times. God called David, "A man after my own heart," yet even he fell under God's judgment. Everything lasting in David's life came because God made an oath of promise without a legal requirement on David's part. God promised to bless

---

[59] Matthew 18:20, Romans 12:5-6

his descendants, and that oath was not dependent on David or his children keeping the law.

Do not use the above passage to think that God will cast us away or take the Holy Spirit from us. Under the Old Covenant, when man was measured by the law, the Spirit could depart. Even when God's prophets were right with Him, the Spirit still came upon them when God was moving. The Spirit could not live within man until sin was taken out of the way. Now we have this promise from **2 Timothy 2:11-13**

> [11] *This is* a faithful saying: For if we died with *Him*, We shall also live with *Him*.
> [12] If we endure, We shall also reign with *Him*. If we deny *Him*, He also will deny us.
> [13] If we are faithless, He remains faithful; He cannot deny Himself.

Notice, even if we are faithless, God remains faithful – for He cannot deny Himself. This is a vital scripture. Your new Spirit is born of God. You are indwelled by God. Once you are in Christ and the Spirit is in you, you are part of God and can never be separated. Remember the passage we read in Ezekiel, which was a foretelling of the New Covenant? God said, "I will create in you a new spirit, and put My Spirit within you."

You are in that covenant now. Once you are born as a child of God's Kingdom, you can never again be denied.

Let's dispel another misconception here. We are told that if we endure, we will reign with Him, but if we deny Him, He will deny us. There was a pastor in the Middle East that was taken from his home in an attempt to convert him back to Islam. His captors dangled him over a cliff and demanded he recant his faith.

This man later testified that he thought about his wife and children, and didn't know how they would survive without him. In that moment of weakness, he recanted.

Many Christians abandoned him and ridiculed him for not being willing to die. I read several comments on this news story where Christians were now calling him an apostate with no hope of salvation. "Jesus will deny him from entering heaven," one commenter posted.

This is completely false. Certainly, we want to remain faithful, even in the face of death, but salvation is not based on your ability to stand in persecution. This passage from 2 Timothy is not talking about salvation at all. It is drawing a comparison.

If we endure, we know we will reign with Christ. This is our highest reward. Jesus said, "To him who overcomes, I will grant to sit with Me on My throne."[60] But to the one who denies Him, that person will be denied that promise. This is not saying that Jesus will deny He ever knew us. It is speaking of being denied the honor promised to those who overcome. And denying Christ is not only our words, but our actions, and our obedience.

Let me give another example. Peter denied he even knew Jesus three times in one night. Yet before he was even tempted, Jesus foretold of Peter's fall. Jesus also said, "But when you return to Me, strengthen your brethren."[61] When Jesus rose from the grave, the first to see Him were the women who went to the tomb to perfume His body. Instead of finding a body, they found the risen Savior. Jesus sent them to tell the disciples, and specifically told them to tell Peter.

It was an act of grace. Though Peter was defeated when his own strength failed him, Jesus did not reject him for denying his faith. Once he became a receiver of the Holy Spirit, he became an overcomer, and because he lived by the power of the Spirit, he never lost courage again. Peter's strength given through the Spirit didn't waver, even when he was being led away to his own crucifixion.

While this doesn't directly apply to our topic, this scripture mentions denial, and it is necessary to dispel fear-based teaching on this topic, so we can go on to faith based truth.

The indwelling Spirit was promised as part of the coming New Covenant, but until sin was removed in Christ, man could not become the temple of God. Look at **John 7:38-39**

---

[60] Revelation 3:31
[61] Luke 22:32

³⁸ "He who believes in Me, as the Scripture has said, out of his heart will flow rivers of living water."

³⁹ But this He spoke concerning the Spirit, whom those believing in Him would receive; for the Holy Spirit was not yet *given*, because Jesus was not yet glorified.

This promise was given before the crucifixion, but the Bible clearly says that these people had this promise, but it could not be fulfilled until after Jesus was glorified through the resurrection. Jesus referred to His death and resurrection as His glorification (see John 12:23-24).

Now we enter Jesus' glory, and by faith we are cleansed through the word, then we receive the abiding presence of Christ through the Holy Spirit. Every believer has the Holy Spirit within them, but this does not equate to being filled with the Spirit. Let's look at a few scriptures to get a bigger picture. First look at **John 20:21-22**

²¹ So Jesus said to them again, "Peace to you! As the Father has sent Me, I also send you."

²² And when He had said this, He breathed on *them*, and said to them, "Receive the Holy Spirit.

Immediately after the resurrection, Jesus came to His disciples and gave them the gift (or indwelling) of the Holy Spirit. Yet right after this, Jesus instructed them to wait in Jerusalem for the power of the Holy Spirit. Look now at **Acts 1:8**

"But you shall receive power when the Holy Spirit has come upon you; and you shall be witnesses to Me in Jerusalem, and in all Judea and Samaria, and to the end of the earth."

They already had the Holy Spirit, for it was given in John 20:22, yet a few days later, Jesus is foretelling of the Spirit coming upon them. This was fulfilled in **Acts 2:1-4**

¹ When the Day of Pentecost had fully come, they were all with one accord in one place.

² And suddenly there came a sound from heaven, as of a

rushing mighty wind, and it filled the whole house where they were sitting.

³ Then there appeared to them divided tongues, as of fire, and *one* sat upon each of them.

⁴ And they were all filled with the Holy Spirit and began to speak with other tongues, as the Spirit gave them utterance.

This is the birth of the church, and it began with the power of the Holy Spirit. Until these men were empowered with the Spirit, their ministry was flat and lifeless. They could have gone out teaching about Jesus and the resurrection, but it would have been the power of personal effort. But when the Spirit came upon them, He turned these inadequate ragtag group of men into powerful ministers of the word.

Now here lies a danger. You cannot put God into a box. As Christians, we tend to believe that how God worked in our life is how God works for everyone. This simply is not true. The first 120 disciples received the gift of the Holy Spirit at the resurrection. This was a separate event than the power of the Holy Spirit, which came 40 days later.

We see a similar event in Acts 8. Philip was sent by God to Samaria. He preached the word and many believed. They were baptized in Jesus' name, and when Peter and John heard of the birth of this new church, they came down. They prayed for the people and laid hands on them. Then the Spirit came upon the new believers with the same power as was at the birth of the church.

However, something different happened in Acts 10, when a soldier named Cornelius gathered his family to hear about the gospel. As Peter preached to them about Jesus Christ, they believed, and the Spirit fell upon them with the same unmistakable signs as at Pentecost, and as occurred at the new church Philip began.

There is a difference in this account. These gentile believers had not been baptized. No one laid hands on them or taught them about the Holy Spirit. Two apostles didn't have to pray for this gift to be given. God showed up and amazed everyone by dismantling their preconceived notions about who God would accept. And He did so without requiring any action on anyone's part.

Cornelius' house received salvation and were filled. Others received salvation and had to pray to receive the power of the Spirit. The point we should take away from this is that God doesn't provide a formula. Once we believe, we can receive. Sometimes God calls us to seek. Sometimes He acts by showing us that He is the one who seeks us.

One thing is certain, the gift of the Spirit is for all. Jesus taught people that if they ask it shall be given, seek and you will find, knock and the door will be opened. These three verbs were spoken in the active present tense in the original Greek. It means to seek, ask, and knock and keep seeking, asking, and knocking. It means to ask with expectation, knowing something will be given.

When I know God's desire is to give, and He says to knock, I'll keep knocking because I know I am guaranteed an answer. I may not yet be ready, but as I answer the call to seek, I am preparing my heart to receive. Once my heart is established in faith, God will open my eyes, and I'll find. And I'll find more than I was expecting, for God says that He gives abundantly above what we think or ask. What's more, when I find, it's only the evidence that there is more to find. The life of seeking should never end. We only quit finding when we quit seeking.

If I'm not receiving the abundant life of the Spirit, I'm not seeking in faith, and therefore am not prepared to receive. All our treasures begin in the Spirit and come through faith. I know the promise is reality; therefore, I seek with expectation. Consider this promise in **Luke 11:13**

"If you then, being evil, know how to give good gifts to your children, how much more will *your* heavenly Father give the Holy Spirit to those who ask Him!"

Remember, the Bible says, "The just shall live by faith." It is not a moment of faith, but a lifestyle of faith. God reveals His word and promises, and as I learn to live in faith, there is no promise or gift out of reach.

Sometimes God uses the miraculous to open our eyes to faith. Other times God teaches us faith before we can see the miraculous. God has no formulas.

Let me give my personal testimony that brought me into this amazing life in the Spirit. I was saved at the age of 13. I was going down the wrong road fast. Nearly every one of my friends I had then ended up in drugs and other substance issues. I even had a friend give me pot seeds. This was about the time God intervened and rescued my soul. I became a new creation, and my outlook changed. I thought I was cool by using as many foul words as I could think of. I boasted in using God's name as a curse word. But in a moment, my mouth changed and I instantly became incompatible with my destructive friendships.

Yet, I had one vice I could not shake. At the age of 9 or so, I had a friend who discovered a payload of pornography. We looked at that trash every day. It was enjoyable until I became a Christian. That is when I swore off porn, but I couldn't break the habit.

It had my mind in such chains that when it called, I could do nothing but obey. It was like a dark fog came over me, and once that desire hit, there was no escape. I would find no relief until I fed the addiction. My mind was being pulled by the bondage of desire, and nothing I did could stop it. One time I was reading my Bible when the dark fog hit. I resisted for a while, but eventually I could think of nothing else. I closed my Bible and sought to gratify my addiction.

It was depressing. If I wasn't even safe when reading the Bible, what hope did I have? I swore off my addictions many times. I promised God I would never do it again more times than I could count. Then in church I would hear, "Look at your sin. If you don't get your life right, God will avenge. Surely your sins will find you out. God is angry at the wicked every day."

I would feel convicted, repent, and then rededicate my life to God again. Sometimes it would last a couple of weeks. One time I made it three months. Sometimes I only made it a few days. When I hit my thirties, I reached my limit. God's wrath was upon me, and there was nothing I could do about it. Since I couldn't beat this thing, I decided to stop trying.

Why bother going to church? All I would hear was condemnation. I knew I was in sin. Telling me how angry God was didn't help anything. It only made things worse. I didn't want to be reminded, so I dropped out of church. I abandoned my faith and decided not to resist my addiction. I indulged myself for the next three to four years. I reasoned that sooner or later I'd quit feeling bad about this if I could stay away from church people.

I poured my life into my career and my addiction. Everyone thought I had it all together, but it was a mask. My career took off, and my turmoil did too. I set a five-year goal for my career, believing this would make me happy. I had landed the job of my dreams, and within a few days my inner life came unglued.

The job didn't bring happiness. I had climbed the mountain of success only to find out nothing was up there. I tried to set a new goal, but I knew that if this didn't make me happy, the next mountain wouldn't either.

I had several days free while my new job waited for a project to start. I tried to study and prepare, but my mind wasn't there. I decided to go to a nearby park and try to pray to the God I left behind. A God I knew was angry, but I didn't know what else to do.

I spent the first day grumbling at the air. The second day was pretty much the same. On the third day, I cried out, "I can't do it. I can't live this Christian life. I can't beat this addiction."

As I walked in the woods and prayed, something miraculous happened. The woods faded from view and a cloud engulfed me. I felt the Holy Spirit pouring into my life. The chains of my addiction literally felt like they came unhooked and fell from my mind. In that instant, I knew my addiction had been broken. Scriptures poured through my mind like a flowing river. Passages I didn't remember came to mind and the gospel suddenly made sense.

Many things flowed through my mind, but one of the most impactful revelations was, "To him who works, his wages are not counted as grace, but as debt. But to him who doesn't work, but believes on Him who justifies the ungodly, his faith is accounted as righteousness."

I have no idea if this experience lasted for a few minutes or a few hours. Time seemed irrelevant. As the woods came back into view, God challenged my heart. He challenged me to prove my revelations against the scriptures. I went home, found a concordance, and started doing word searches. Everything God showed me was affirmed in the word.

God made it clear this wasn't for myself alone, but He was calling me to minister to others. Then God called me to release my career and trust Him with my job and finances.

For the next three months, my head was buzzing. It took some time for my thoughts to begin to settle and become clear. Before this day, I hated writing. It was the most dreaded task in school. After this, I had the overwhelming desire to express what God was showing me into written words. I sat down and wrote a dozen pages. Then another idea would grow and I'd have to write it out. I wrote out my addiction story and shared it with my wife. She knew something was wrong, but had no idea about what I was going through.

I had been called to preach at 13, but nothing I taught or preached had any power. At 32, God affirmed my calling, and suddenly people were responding. I've gone through many things, but as I learned to focus on Christ and the word, the scriptures began to come alive.

There is much more to this story, but what I hope the reader takes away from this is the power of the Spirit. Without the Spirit poured out upon me, I couldn't defeat sin. Without this power, my ministry was dead – even during the times I was able to restrain my sin.

The perceived anger of God drove me into darkness, but at the most sinful time of my life, God showed me favor beyond anything I could have imagined. I would have been happy breaking my addiction, but God broke my addiction and poured His life into me, and gave me the satisfying life of writing, ministering, and learning how to discover the inexhaustible depths of the word. As an extra blessing, He also blessed my career in ways I could not have expected.

Some call this the baptism of the Holy Spirit, but one thing is certain, I received Christ when I was 13. My life changed and my faith was unmistakable. But I received power from on high when I was 32. From 13 to 32, my efforts were in the flesh. But when the Spirit was poured out in my life, my real journey of faith began.

Some claim the evidence of the Spirit is speaking in tongues. I did not speak in tongues. I've spent many weeks praying and seeking the truth about tongues. God made it clear this is not for my life. The Bible calls tongues a gift of the Spirit. But it also says there is a diversity of gifts. The same Spirit, but different gifts. Then the Bible says in **1 Corinthians 12:7-11,30**

> [7] But the manifestation of the Spirit is given to each one for the profit *of all*:
> [8] for to one is given the word of wisdom through the Spirit, to another the word of knowledge through the same Spirit,
> [9] to another faith by the same Spirit, to another gifts of healings by the same Spirit,
> [10] to another the working of miracles, to another prophecy, to another discerning of spirits, to another *different* kinds of tongues, to another the interpretation of tongues.
> [11] But one and the same Spirit works all these things, distributing to each one individually as He wills.
>
> ...
>
> [30] Do all have gifts of healings? Do all speak with tongues? Do all interpret?

The Bible clearly teaches that every spiritual gift comes from the same Holy Spirit, but He distributes to each person in the church individually as He wills. The Bible explains that the gifts of the Spirit are designed so that each member edifies the entire church.

Then the Bible asks a redundant question. Do all speak in tongues? Do all have the gift of healings? The answer is, "No." The gifts are distributed as the Spirit chooses. So why do some in the church claim that everyone must have tongues?

Many times, when I mention that I don't speak in tongues, people in some church circles tell me that I don't have the Holy Spirit. Where does the Bible say this? Scripture teaches just the opposite. Are we allowing pet doctrines to cause us to deny the working of the Spirit? Can I look at my experience and the evidence of the Spirit's work and say, "That wasn't the Holy Spirit. I won't accept this unless God conforms to my expectation through tongues?"

Some claim that tongues and the gifts of the Spirit ceased in the first century. This is also false. The problem is that some do not believe, and without faith there is no way to receive. Even my life testifies to this. I prayed for decades for deliverance, but they were faithless prayers. Yet in my broken state, when I fully understood that I could not overcome, God revealed His power to me, and with joy I received. My religion blinded me. Then my pursuit of self-gratification blinded me. But when everything was stripped away, the revelation of faith began.

Some don't receive because they don't believe, and others fake the gifts because they believe in self-effort tongues. But the Bible says that the Spirit gave them utterance.

I do believe the gifts of the Spirit are just as relevant today as it was at Pentecost. But if we are trying to mimic the Spirit, it's not a gift of the Spirit; it's the gift of the flesh through human effort.

Tongues are not mentioned until the eighth gift. Why then do people in the church make it the vital gift that supposedly IS the evidence we have the Spirit? The fruit of the Spirit is the only evidence we have been given as a tangible measurement. I know several people who say they speak and pray in tongues, and their lives show the evidence of spiritual maturity and faith. I know many who supposedly speak in tongues, but have no fruit in their lives. Just because someone falls out, does not mean the Holy Spirit is upon them. Just because someone speaks in a way that can't be understood, doesn't mean they are speaking in tongues as the Spirit gives them utterance.

As a young teen, I went to a lake-side worship service with about fifty people. It wasn't long before people were speaking in tongues and falling on the ground.

A young man I knew fell out, and was staggering so badly, he had to be dragged home. Many of those people who spoke in tongues and fell out are people I still know. I saw their lives over several decades. Many fell into drugs, became promiscuous, became alcoholics, and many don't even claim to be Christians anymore.

Does this mean all similar experiences are false signs? No. For every move of God, there is a counterfeit. If you read in the book of Revelation, in the last days power will be given to false prophets to perform miracles. See Revelation 13:13-14 and 16:14. These signs are how spirits of wickedness deceive those who do not believe. Even Jesus warned of this in Matthew 24:24 and Mark 13:22.

These become a distraction for believers and a deception to unbelievers. Add to this, lying signs cause people to reject the Spirit, believing that all evidence is false. The one evidence that they are not of God is that the signs become the focus, and more glory is given to the worker, and less focus is on Christ. The true working of the Spirit will always point to Christ and bear the fruit of the Spirit.

I stood there, looking around with another one of my cousins, and we were the only two standing. I mourned over the fact that God had touched everyone but us. Why not me?

Now I look back and compare my Holy Spirit experience with what I saw that night. My life drastically changed. The power of God transformed me. My ministry has been growing. My love for the word and the Lord continues to grow. I can't look back without seeing how much I am growing each day, week, month, and year. Why would being baptized in the Spirit drive sin out of my life, but have no effect on the mass of people I witnessed?

Why is the evidence of the Spirit so strong in my life, but it's scoffed at because I didn't speak in tongues. Why are people whose lives show no evidence of change authenticated because they did speak in tongues? I believe it's because Christians are being taught to look at the wrong things. We've put the Spirit in a box.

The Charismatic churches limit the Spirit by deciding what they will accept as evidence, not even considering the Bible's teaching that we will know by their fruit. The Holy Spirit is the only one that can produce the fruit of the Spirit. Fruit can be counterfeited on the surface, but when that person is shaken, any fruit that is not eternal will be shaken away and proven as a work of the flesh.

Non-Charismatic churches limit the Spirit by denying the gifts. They put the Spirit in a box by deciding what is acceptable and what is not. They pray, "Holy Spirit, have your way," but He doesn't move because what they mean is, "You are free to operate only in ways we are comfortable with."

The truth is, God divides gifts as He wills. Everyone is promised the gift of the Holy Spirit. The empowering of the Spirit, or baptism of the Spirit, is not to a select few, but to the entire church. But the gifts are not to every believer. If allowed to be received, every gift edifies the entire church, but that does not mean that every member has the same gift. The Bible is clear that the Spirit divides the gifts individually as He wills.

Tongues is a gift given to whomever the Spirit chooses. It is not better than the gift of prophecy (the proclamation of the word). Each gift (Word of wisdom, word of knowledge, faith, healings, working of miracles, prophecy, discernment, tongues, interpretation of tongues) is part of God's edification of the entire body. My gift of the word is not lesser than someone's gift of tongues. Nor does my gift devalue someone else's gift. The Spirit distributes gifts in ways that will edify the body of believers.

It's time to stop putting a denominational spin on the word, and let truth be truth. Individual gifts are not for everyone, but the filling of the Spirit is for all. Look at **Ephesians 5:17-21**

> [17] Therefore do not be unwise, but understand what the will of the Lord *is*.
>
> [18] And do not be drunk with wine, in which is dissipation; but be filled with the Spirit,
>
> [19] speaking to one another in psalms and hymns and

spiritual songs, singing and making melody in your heart to the Lord,

[20] giving thanks always for all things to God the Father in the name of our Lord Jesus Christ,

[21] submitting to one another in the fear of God.

Don't be unwise. You have specific things the Bible reveals as the will of the Lord for your life. Being filled with the Spirit is for each person. And tongues is not even mentioned. When we are filled with the Spirit, it will produce edification. Psalms, hymns, songs, and a joyful and thankful heart is the evidence of the natural flow of the Spirit. The Spirit glorifies Christ, so the one filled will have the desire to give thanks in the name of Christ.

It is my belief that each Christian has the invitation to be baptized in the Spirit. The Bible says there is one body, one Spirit, one Lord, one faith, and one baptism.[62] The Bible also says that through Jesus, we are baptized with the Holy Spirit.[63] When you see the Spirit falling upon a believer, you never see it repeated. The Bible only mentions this once with the apostles and those in the upper room. When they went to a city that received the gospel, you see them being instrumental tools of God in the one baptism for that place. There isn't a single place where the Spirit fell upon someone or a group twice.

Being filled with the Spirit is a continuous process. In Acts, when the church was threatened by the political powers, they gathered and prayed for God's power. Let's look at how the Bible answers this prayer in **Acts 4:31**

And when they had prayed, the place where they were assembled together was shaken; and they were all filled with the Holy Spirit, and they spoke the word of God with boldness.

In this event, tongues is absent. Miracles are absent. Signs and wonders are absent. What is present is the power of the Holy Spirit to speak the word of God with boldness.

---

[62] Ephesians 4:5
[63] Matthew 3:11

Filled with the Spirit

In Ephesians 5 above, the command to be filled is in the present passive tense. It is the continuous act of filling to the top, and the work is not by the person being filled. We are being continuously filled with the Spirit. This is why the Just shall live by faith. We live this Christian life by faith, trusting in the Spirit to fill us. When we stop seeking and receiving, we'll begin to feel dry. That is the call to return our eyes to Christ, pray with expectation, and allow the Spirit to fill us to the top. This is power for living. This is power for ministry. Without this filling, we only have human effort as our strength.

Being filled again is only mentioned here in Ephesians. It is in response to being distracted by worldliness. It is in response to those who are acting without wisdom (verse 15), redeeming our time in this world (verse 16), and not allowing ourselves to lose sight of God's will (verse 17). Instead of seeking comfort from wine, we are filled with the source of true comfort and power, the Holy Spirit.

This act of being filled counteracts the worldly thinking in verses 14-18, and empowers us to edify the church, do ministry, and fulfill God's plan in our families – verses 19-28.

The Holy Spirit is the power to transform our lives, the power to edify the church, the power to strengthen the family, and the power to evangelize the world around us. Without the transformation of the Spirit and a continuous renewal, most of our work will be in the flesh, and have limited success at best.

Be filled. If you lack this power, ask with expectation, seek knowing you will find, and knock believing God has given you the invitation. Don't stop seeking until the promise becomes reality. This promise is for you!

Discussion Questions

Review John 7:38-39. Is this promise to every believer?

Read John 20:22, Luke 24:49-51, Acts 1:8, and Acts 2:1-4. When did the disciples receive the Holy Spirit?

When did the disciples show evidence of the power of the Spirit, when they received the Spirit in John, or when they received the power from on high in Acts?

Read Acts 10:24-27, 10:43-47, Acts 8:14-17, and Romans 10:9-10. Where the people in Acts 8 saved?

Read 1 John 3:9, 1 Corinthians 3:16 and Acts 2:21. Does a saved person have the Holy Spirit within them? Is the signs of the Spirit required by the Bible for us to be saved?

Is the power of the Holy Spirit (sometimes called the baptism of the Spirit) always at the time of salvation?

Why does the Bible have such varying accounts on the baptism of the Spirit?

Review 1 Corinthians 12:7-11. How many gifts of the Spirit are mentioned here?

Does the Bible say that any of these gifts are required as evidence we have the Spirit?

Which of these gifts does the Bible say is the most important?

Read 1 Corinthians 14:1-5. Prophesying (or proclaiming the truths of the word) is listed as the most important gift to the church. Does the Christian get to choose this gift?

What is the difference between being baptized in the Spirit (receiving power from on high) and being continuously filled with the Spirit?

Spiritual Warfare

Spiritual warfare is another topic that is often misunderstood. While the Bible declares our victory, many teach oppression. The Bible teaches that Jesus defeated ALL principalities on the cross, but many teach that we must fight to defeat spiritual oppression.

Any doctrine that teaches fear is not of faith. Any doctrine that does not teach us how to stand firm in the victory that has already been given to us is a false teaching. People who teach these things may be very sincere, but fear-based teaching is still untrue. Satan cannot overcome a Christian. Demons cannot possess a Christian. In fact, Satan and demons cannot even oppress a Christian. As you will soon see, the Bible clearly teaches these things. A good starting point is **1 John 4:4**

You are of God, little children, and have overcome them, because He who is in you is greater than he who is in the world.

This scripture follows our promise that we have the ability to know what spirit is of God, and we can identify what is contrary to Christ. The power within you, the Holy Spirit, is greater than any power the world can send against you. Satan may come against the believer, but we have already overcome. Those who stand by faith negate the worldly power of any spirit of oppression, deception, and all principalities.

Also, the Bible never tells the Christian to bind Satan, rebuke Satan, or even fight against Satan. We are called to stand firm on the rock of victory. There is no war to win – other than that which wages against our minds, which is sin within our own flesh.[64]

What most people claim is satanic oppression is their own desires. Our enemy tries to lure us into defeat by persuading us to set our minds back on the flesh. If he can't get you to become

---

[64] Romans 7:20-23

fleshly minded through lusts, he will try to deceive you into serving religion through the flesh.

Satan laughs when Christians are taught to trust in their own words. When someone says, "Get thee behind me, Satan," he has gained a temporary victory. For that Christian has taken their eyes off Christ and they are no longer trusting in the complete victory of Christ. They are now focused on trying to accomplish in their own efforts what Jesus has already done.

There is a difference between confessing our promises and trying to beat Satan with our words. One is proclaiming our faith in what God has accomplished, and confessing the reality of the promise. The other is someone trying to use the power of their own words because they believe they must do, instead of believing it is finished. One speaks to the mountain to be moved based on what God has already accomplished, the other is trying to carve a path that does not yet exist. One is faith, the other is the confession of a false belief that man can accomplish what God has already done. Then our words are nothing but acts of the flesh.

God will never empower you to accomplish what Jesus has already done. He calls us to trust in the completed work of Christ, but the Lord does not bless your attempts to duplicate the work of Christ. When we try to become our own victory, we are making ourselves a rival of Jesus. The devil will twist the scriptures to persuade us that God's grace is ONLY something that gives us the power to do God-like works through our own efforts. He does not want you to believe that you stand in what Jesus has already done.

Romans 5:2 tells us that faith in God causes us to stand, and we have hope in the glory of God. We stand by faith, not by human effort. Or as **1 Corinthians 4:20** states:

For the kingdom of God *is* not in word but in power.

Confession is a declaration of our faith in what God has accomplished. Then it is not our words, but our faith. We are receivers of God's power as we enter into it by faith. To those who think it is their words, the Bible says, it is not through your words, but by God's power. Trusting in your words is idolatry. Confessing your confidence in God's power is worship. One is the mind set on the things of the Spirit, the other is the mind trusting in the flesh, which is the things of this earth. Look at **Colossians 3:2-3**

2 Set your mind on things above, not on things on the earth.

3 For you died, and your life is hidden with Christ in God.

Temptation that masquerades as religion calls you to take your eyes off that which is above, and focus on the things of this life. The truth is, the more we become receivers of the things of promise, the more the fountain of grace through the Spirit in us flows out and affects the world around us.

If your life is hidden with Christ in God, how can Satan possess or oppress? Can Satan storm the gates of heaven, overthrow God and bind Christ so he can now oppress you? No, this is impossible. Not only that, but Jesus said the opposite is true. The gates of hell, which is Satan's strongest defense, cannot stand before the church.[65] A gate is something our enemy erects because he is attempting to protect himself.

Since Satan cannot stand against the church, he uses deception. He persuades the members of the church that they need to be fighting in their own strength. He persuades us to fight against each other, he tells us that we need to fight against ourselves, and he also distracts us with the cares of this life.

Have you seen someone panic when they think there is a spider on them? Even if there is no spider, they will jump around, thrash, and even run away. They might lock themselves in a bathroom and strip down to look for a spider that isn't there. This is what the church is doing through most teachings on spiritual warfare.

Let's first dispel a few myths so we can see the truths of scripture without distraction. The first thing to note is that the war of temptation is not against Satan. It's against your own flesh. The devil might provoke your flesh because he knows it will become your focus, but sin is in the flesh. It is not a spiritual battle.

When the Apostle Paul spoke about his struggles with sin, he never once mentioned the devil. He made it clear that the real

---

[65]Matthew 16:18

battle was learning how to set his mind on the Spirit by focusing on Christ. When his mind was in the flesh, he could do nothing but serve the law of sin. Look at **Romans 7:23-25**

> [23] But I see another law in my members, warring against the law of my mind, and bringing me into captivity to the law of sin which is in my members.
>
> [24] O wretched man that I am! Who will deliver me from this body of death?
>
> [25] I thank God-- through Jesus Christ our Lord! So then, with the mind I myself serve the law of God, but with the flesh the law of sin.

He doesn't rebuke Satan. He turns to Christ. Once Paul learned to trust in Christ during his times of weakness, he discovered that the mind on the Spirit could do nothing but serve the law of God. It was a natural result of the mind focused on Christ. But the mind on the flesh can do nothing but serve the law of sin.

This is true whether we are pursuing lustful flesh or religious flesh. Lustful flesh promises us that we can be satisfied through our flesh without the need for God. Religious flesh promises us that we can be satisfied with our own self-righteousness, without needing God's gift of righteousness. We can become righteous independent of God. There is no difference. These are two ends of the same spectrum.

I've counseled countless Christians who were defeated by self-imposed guilt because they had a sinful thought. No doubt their thoughts were sinful, for the Bible says, "Whatever is not of faith is sin."[66] Every thought that originates from the flesh is sin, but we only recognize the ones we think are bad.

Then Satan manipulates Christians by telling them the imaginary spider is on their back through words of condemnation. You have committed the unpardonable sin. You thought blasphemy. You thought about revenge. On and on it goes. He is provoking the flesh, and the Christian who is trying to live out their lives in the flesh are powerless to stand against this imaginary guilt

---

[66] Romans 14:23

and condemnation. If we believe the spider of oppression is real, we'll live as if it is real.

Many are living under Christian voodoo. The pagan cultures that practice voodoo have a secret to their power. The person being cursed has to know they are being cursed. This is why an enemy tacks a doll to their door. It is necessary for the cursed person to see this, for until they know they are being targeted, voodoo has no power.

When voodoo curses those who then shrug it off as a silly superstition, the curse loses its power. The reason is that it has no power outside of the faith people have in this imaginary superstition.

In the same way, many Christians who are weak in faith may be convinced they are under the curse of sin, or the oppression of Satan. Because they believe in the curse, they will be tormented by it. For every gift of God, there is a counterfeit of the flesh. When we put our trust in the things of the flesh (including the curse of sin), this causes us to disbelieve in the gifts through the Spirit.

Though the Bible says that Jesus became a curse for us, and the curse came to an end in Christ, this promise has no effect to the person who trusts more in oppression than they do in Christ. Though the Bible says that all principalities and powers of wickedness were disarmed and defeated on the cross, to the person who trusts more in Satan's boasting than they do in Christ, this promise has no effect. It's not the promise that has lost effect, but without faith, the promise is pushed aside.

For the Christian, there is no such thing as an unpardonable sin. I've discussed this in detail in my other books, so I won't rehash it here, but just stop and look at who Jesus was speaking to. It was those who were rejecting Christ and rebelling against the Spirit of Grace. Any who deny the Spirit and refuse to allow themselves to be changed into a new creation, cannot have forgiveness in the life to come because salvation is only through Christ. And the Spirit they were calling the worker of Satan is what draws them to Christ.

Bad thoughts (including blasphemous ones) cannot defeat the accomplished work of Christ. Yet those who fear thoughts are disbelieving God's promise that sin has already been defeated. And He doesn't stop there. God then works in us to drive sin out of our life through the power of the Spirit.

You will never get your thought life under control if you are focusing on yourself. The Bible says that if we walk in the Spirit, we will not fulfill the lusts of the flesh.[67] The power of the flesh is stripped away by the life of the Spirit. Stop trying to overcome sin. That is God's job. Read Micah 7:19. God subdues our iniquities. You can't use the flesh of human effort to defeat the desires of human flesh.

God has told us how to cast down our thoughts. And it is not by focusing on Satan. Look at **2 Corinthians 10:4-5**

4 For the weapons of our warfare *are* not carnal but mighty in God for pulling down strongholds,

5 casting down arguments and every high thing that exalts itself against the knowledge of God, bringing every thought into captivity to the obedience of Christ,

The weapons of spiritual warfare are not carnal (or physical). The might is in God, not in us. And how do we cast down that which exalts itself against God? Through the obedience of Christ. Not our obedience to Christ, but the obedience Christ has accomplished for us. It is by faith. All things in the Spirit are received by faith. Jesus has declared our victory through Him, and as God reveals this to us, He also calls us to trust in His work.

The enemy tries to defeat us by telling us we need to be obedient, instead of trusting in Christ's obedience. He knows that as we have faith in Jesus' work, we become receivers of that work, and the same obedience Jesus accomplished begins emerging in our life. So the spirit of deception just gives a slight twist. "You must be more obedient," the enemy says.

The spiritual warfare is the battle between trusting in Christ and walking by faith, or trusting in physical things and walking by human effort. Let's add another powerful passage to this. Look now at **James 1:14-16**

---

[67] Galatians 5:16

¹⁴ But each one is tempted when he is drawn away by his own desires and enticed.

¹⁵ Then, when desire has conceived, it gives birth to sin; and sin, when it is full-grown, brings forth death.

¹⁶ Do not be deceived, my beloved brethren.

If your church background is similar to mine, you have been taught that when YOU resist Satan he flees from you. That is a lie. Once again, the deceiver has slightly twisted this scripture just enough so you miss the mark. You don't have to be far off, just enough to keep you out of faith. The passage that speaks about resisting the devil is not talking about mere human resistance, but is teaching you to trust in the power of God.

First, the Bible is again saying what we read in Romans. Temptation is your own flesh desiring something that lures you away from God. Stop blaming the devil. Don't say God has tempted you. It is your own desires. The devil may dangle what he knows you desire in your sight, but he has no power to drive you toward temptation. He is standing to the side calling out for you to look. God unveils His promises and calls for you to keep your eyes on Christ. James explains how we are tempted, now let's look at how James explains how we escape temptation. **James 4:7-8**

⁷ Therefore submit to God. Resist the devil and he will flee from you.

⁸ Draw near to God and He will draw near to you. Cleanse *your* hands, *you* sinners; and purify *your* hearts, *you* double-minded.

Is the focus on resisting Satan? I was once taught that when you resist sin, Satan has to flee. This was confusing because when I was resisting, I never felt relief. Temptation would keep pounding my will through my mind until I was at a point of weakness, and then I would give in.

The focus is not on your resistance, but God's power. God calls for you to turn to Him. When we answer that call, we draw near to God, and when our minds are drawn into the Spirit where God is always near, Satan has to flee. Satan cannot abide in God's presence. All he can do is lure us back into a fleshly mind where he has the advantage.

The book of James then instructs us to be pure. In this passage, the Christian is not being called a sinner as in that being our identity. The Bible clearly teaches that our new spirit cannot sin.[68] The Greek word 'hamartolos' means someone devoted to sin, or someone with sinful vices. It can refer to either a believer or unbeliever, for it is speaking of someone who is unable to stop committing the same sins. Add to this his rebuke of being double-minded. This means to waiver back and forth with uncertainty.

Have you ever met a great man or woman of faith that wavered with uncertainty about the victory they have in Christ? No. The reason they are strong in the faith is because they don't waver from their certainty of God's gift of victory.

The person struggling with sin is almost always someone who doubts God's power in them. They doubt God's forgiveness. They doubt God's promise that they are always accepted because they are in Christ. They doubt God's promise (and command) to come confidently before God's throne of grace when they are in need – which is when they have sinned.

On the other hand, the more someone steps out of double-mindedness and becomes confident in the finished work of Christ and the gift of grace, their faith begins drawing them out of sin and negative ways of thinking.

Finally, James tells us to purify our hearts. Again, this is impossible by human effort. This is by faith in Christ alone. When the Apostle Peter first preached to the Gentiles and saw the miracle of life through the Spirit poured out upon them, he said, "God made no distinction between them and ourselves, purifying their hearts by faith."[69]

This is a call to step into the life of faith, which is how we draw near to God, and receive the promise that God draws near to us,

---

[68] 1 John 3:9, 1 Peter 1:23
[69] Acts 15:9

draws us out of temptation, suppresses our iniquities (or sinful habits), and empowers us to be receivers of the fruit of the Spirit.

Spiritual warfare is a limited warfare. Satan can't overthrow the Christian's faith. Nor can he remove God's gift of righteousness. Nor can he stop the church from conquering every stronghold he has in this world. Since this is true, he twists scriptures and tries to confuse us into abandoning faith so we are no longer receivers of the fruit of the Spirit. And he has done a very effective job. Christians are so focused on their sins that they are paralyzed and incapable of walking in the Spirit. The devil has persuaded the church to trust in their own obedience instead of the obedience of Christ.

He convinces the church to fight for victory, knowing that if people are beating the air with their words and works, they will be ignorant of the victory that has already been given. Look at the promise of **1 John 5:4**

For whatever is born of God overcomes the world. And this is the victory that has overcome the world-- our faith.

How do we obtain the victory and overcome the world? We don't. Jesus said, "Be of good cheer, I have overcome the world."[70] Now we enter that victory through faith. Notice, this is the victory that HAS (past tense) overcome the world. We are not trying to overcome. By faith we are entering into the victory Christ has already accomplished for us. By faith, we become receivers of Christ's work. Let's bring in **Colossians 2:15-19**

[15] Having disarmed principalities and powers, He made a public spectacle of them, triumphing over them in it.

[16] So let no one judge you in food or in drink, or regarding a festival or a new moon or sabbaths,

[17] which are a shadow of things to come, but the substance is of Christ.

[18] Let no one cheat you of your reward, taking delight in *false* humility and worship of angels, intruding into those things which he has not seen, vainly puffed up by his fleshly mind,

---

[70] John 16:33

^{19} and not holding fast to the Head, from whom all the body, nourished and knit together by joints and ligaments, grows with the increase *that is* from God.

I wanted to bring in more of this scripture so we can see it in a larger context. I encourage you to read this entire chapter of Colossians. It first explains that Christ crucified our flesh nature, took our sins out of the way, and took the law that condemned us out of the way by nailing it to the cross. Not only that, but on the cross Jesus disarmed and triumphed over all principalities.

Satan is one of those principalities. Stop and meditate on this vital truth. Satan has been disarmed. What power does he have against you? Jesus triumphed over the devil, and we enter Jesus' victory by faith. What are we trying to defeat?

There is nothing to defeat, for the victory has already been won. But with that victory we have been given a warning. "Don't let anyone cheat you." People are deceived into believing they have to win a war that has come to an end with our enemy's total defeat. They are deceived into believing that we must try to gain God's acceptance and overcome our sins through keeping the Sabbath, keeping festivals (such as the feast days of the Old Covenant), or keeping legalistic requirements of food, drink, or abstaining from certain foods or drinks.

The Bible clearly says that these were shadows of what was to come but not the actual substance. They pointed to Christ. Now that He has fulfilled all things, we are fulfillers of all requirements by trusting in Christ. We enter into His finished work by faith, and are accounted as obedient through Him.

I know a pastor that teaches that the church and Christians cannot be blessed unless they keep the feast days. His justification is that in Leviticus 23, the Bible says these are to be kept forever. His reasoning is that if this is true, then Christ doesn't bring an end to these ordinances of the law, because then the Bible would be wrong in saying forever.

The problem is that we are putting our English words in place of this scripture, which was written in Hebrew. There is no word in

Hebrew for forever. Let me state that again. There is no word in Hebrew that means forever. The Hebrew word is 'owlam', which means: long duration, perpetual, continuous, or indefinite.

Let me give a couple of quick examples of how the Bible uses this word that proves this doesn't mean never-ending. Look at **Leviticus 7:34b**

I have given them to Aaron the priest and to his sons from the children of Israel by a statute forever.'

Aaron was the brother of Moses, and God made him and his sons the priests of Israel. Then God made it a perpetual priesthood with the promise above. Over the next few generations, the descendants of Aaron became wicked and used the office of the priest for personal gain. Then God stripped away the priesthood in **1 Samuel 2:30**

"Therefore the LORD God of Israel says: 'I said indeed *that* your house and the house of your father would walk before Me forever.' But now the LORD says:
'Far be it from Me; for those who honor Me I will honor, and those who despise Me shall be lightly esteemed.'

The Lord goes on to say that He will cut off all the descendants of Aaron and will give the priesthood to the prophet Samuel. The word 'forever' which means 'perpetual', does not mean that God cannot bring something to an end. It means that something cannot end until God brings it to an end.

There are many commands that God gave as a perpetual ordinance. It wasn't just the feast days. The wave offering taken from the sacrifices was an ordinance forever (owlam). In Leviticus 16, God said His people were to afflict their souls as a remembrance of their sins and make an atoning sacrifice. This ordinance was to be forever (owlam). Yet the Bible clearly tells us that it is a sin against Christ to return to the atoning animal sacrifices that once pointed to Him.

The temptation to abandon faith in Christ is part of our spiritual warfare. Satan uses human fleshly reasoning to twist the scriptures in ways that nullify the completed work of Christ. Then the power of the gospel is made of no effect, for we are then deceived into trusting in ordinances instead of Christ.

Don't allow anyone to put you back under the law with these things. These all pointed to Christ but had no substance. They were a foreshadow, but Jesus is the substance. Once the real thing came through Christ, to return back to these ordinances is disobedience, not obedience.

You and I are in victory when we are in Christ. Spiritual warfare is real, but we are fighting a defeated enemy. In the 1970s and 80s, several South American countries experienced defeat in war. The defeated regimes lost their authority and power, but they continued fighting through guerrilla warfare. They would hide in the jungles and come out to do surprise attacks. Their goal was to destabilize the governments they hated.

In a nutshell, this is our spiritual warfare. Our enemy is defeated, but he hides in the shadows. When he sees an opportunity to destabilize us, he attacks. Then when he sees we are able to resist through faith, he retreats. With this information in mind, let's conclude this chapter by looking at how the Bible explains spiritual warfare in **Ephesians 6:12-17**

12 For we do not wrestle against flesh and blood, but against principalities, against powers, against the rulers of the darkness of this age, against spiritual *hosts* of wickedness in the heavenly *places*.

13 Therefore take up the whole armor of God, that you may be able to withstand in the evil day, and having done all, to stand.

14 Stand therefore, having girded your waist with truth, having put on the breastplate of righteousness,

15 and having shod your feet with the preparation of the gospel of peace;

16 above all, taking the shield of faith with which you will be able to quench all the fiery darts of the wicked one.

17 And take the helmet of salvation, and the sword of the Spirit, which is the word of God;

This begins just as we read earlier – the weapons of our warfare are not carnal, but mighty in God. Though Satan fires off his fiery darts at our flesh, the battle is not fought and cannot be won in the flesh. It's a spiritual battle. We can be deceived into thinking it is in the flesh, but that is so we are tricked into fighting in the flesh where there is no promise of victory. Spiritual victory cannot be obtained in the flesh. However, victory over the flesh CAN be obtained through the Spirit. The Spirit has power over the flesh, but the flesh has no power over the life of the Spirit. This is true whether we are trying to do good or bad.

Don't forget that we are fighting wicked principalities in high places, but the Bible has already assured us that Jesus disarmed and triumphed over them. Satan cannot attack your spirit. He cannot oppress or possess. So though he is a spiritual being, he is reduced to employing the flesh to do his bidding. If he can't directly assault us with our flesh, he will use other fleshly minded people in an attempt to shake our faith.

As we examined earlier, Satan uses our flesh to war against our minds. The weapons of his warfare are carnal, but ours are not. He uses your weaknesses to draw you out of faith. Once you aren't walking in faith, you are warring according to the flesh. Our enemy also uses other people of the flesh in his tactics. If he can use envy, jealousy, hatred, or other fleshly tools, he will stir up people against us.

This is a masterful tactic, for if someone wrongs us, we are immediately tempted to fall back into the flesh and return fire. There can be no victory when we fall back to our own human resources. This is why you see wars in the church, or Christians that previously seemed gentle become aggressive and hostile. Once our pride is hurt, if we are in the flesh, we will go to war to regain self-esteem.

But the Bible steps in to say, "Your weapon is not in the flesh, but is spiritual and mighty in God and not in yourself." And the enemy of your warfare might appear to be another person of the flesh, but the reality is that this is a spiritual battle that must be handled through faith and not self-defense or self-offense.

This is when we are instructed to take on the whole armor of God. These are the things God has issued to us through His gift of grace. Also take note that you are not fighting Satan. You are standing firm. You are already in a position of victory, but now you have been equipped by God to stand. Spiritual warfare is the enemy's attempt to draw you out of victory. It is not you trying to obtain victory.

When the Apostle Paul wrote this, he was looking at a Roman soldier's armor and seeing its parallel to the Christian's defense. The belt around the waist held everything together. In the same way, our understanding of truth holds everything in our spiritual life together. When we know truth, we are prepared for battle.

Satan attacks us with condemnation and tries to pierce our heart with claims that we are no longer accepted by God. He points at our failures and uses that to destroy our fellowship of agape love with our Lord. But God's gift of righteousness guards our heart. We have God's promises that we can never again be brought under condemnation, and even when we sin, because we are under Christ's righteousness, we can confidently come to the throne of grace without fear or dread. Righteousness is based on God's faithfulness, and when we grasp the truth that we are accepted because we are in Christ, these attacks cannot penetrate to our heart.

Our feet are guarded with the gospel of peace. The Roman soldier did not wear steel coverings as most armies of that day did. Their reasoning was that if they were lighter on their feet and could get a firm foundation, they had an advantage over the enemy. They wore sandals with metal cleats to grip the ground and straps to secure the shoe. The strap secured the ankle all the way up to the knee. Their feet were not going to slide.

Because we have the peace of God that goes beyond human understanding, and with it God guards our minds and secures us in His grace, the enemy will not be able to push us off our place of victory.

The shield of faith is to quench the fiery darts of the enemy. Roman soldiers did not carry heavy metal shields. They stayed as light as possible so they didn't tire from carrying the equipment, and could be light and agile. Opposing armies would shoot flaming arrows at the soldiers. Since their shields were wooden, they would soak them in water before battle. Then when the fiery arrow hit the shield, the flames were quenched.

In the same way, we are immersed in the Spirit. When the attacks come, they are quickly quenched and become harmless. But there is a problem in many Christian circles.

When someone isn't secured with the belt of truth, and they don't know why they believe, there is a temptation to become a shield for our faith. When faith is a human attribute, it is artificial and fragile. When someone has a fragile faith, they try to protect their faith from challengers instead of allowing faith to become their shield.

Many Christians stand in front of their faith and fight off challenges with human reasoning. When that fails, they draw out the clubs of emotions. This is especially true when pet doctrines are treated as though they are divine. If someone is grounded in the truth and guarded by the armor of God, emotions don't become the defense of the gospel. Because we have the word of truth, we can rest in peace while assessing every teaching, objection, or question.

To give an example, my wife was friends with another Christian she met through a discussion group. At first, the friendship went well, but then my wife expressed questions about some of the things this woman believed. My wife also confessed that at times she struggles with doubt and wanted to understand if the topic at hand was true. Instead of opening the scriptures and sharing why something was true, or seeing if some of her beliefs might not be anchored in scripture, she lashed out with anger. She sent my wife a letter saying she could no longer be friends. She ended by saying, "You have a disease called doubt. I must avoid doubters or else I might catch your disease."

Is faith the absence of doubt? No. Faith assures us in the face of doubt. This reaction showed that she had a fragile faith that wasn't grounded in truth. She didn't think her faith could stand, so she stood as a shield to her faith, protecting it at all cost, while pretending her own questions didn't exist.

This is not biblical faith. Faith is the assurance of truth. It is the evidence of our hope. It isn't a denial of reality, and faith is not dependent upon me squelching any threat before it can reach my faith. Faith is not a weak belief system I must protect and insulate from the disease of doubt. Quite the opposite. True faith quenches doubt. It is the things that cause doubt that are threatened, not faith.

Human faith is built upon emotions and the carnal intellect. It must be protected. Biblical faith is the revelation of God's truth with the invitation to believe and put our trust in what the Spirit is revealing. Then faith shields us. It needs no shield, for it is the power of God unveiled to our life in the Spirit. But that is only understood as we learn to trust fully in Christ, and learn to walk in the fellowship of the Spirit.

If I am experiencing fellowship with my Creator, have witnessed the power of His transforming life, and am continuing to receive from the Holy Spirit given to me, no challenge of doubt can persuade me to disbelieve in what is an undeniable reality. The fiery darts of the devil can't make me doubt what I have seen and experienced. I can't doubt what I know to be real.

We have also been given the helmet of salvation. You have the assurance of salvation to protect you when Satan attempts to make you doubt your life in the Spirit. A human based salvation causes doubt, for when my performance falters, I will lose confidence. But to the one who understands that salvation is a gift, and believes God's promise that His gifts and callings are irrevocable,[71] we will have peace even when our performance fails. This peace of God guards our hearts and minds through Christ.

Keep in mind that doubt is not the absence of faith. Many teach that if we have doubts, we are sinners in God's eyes. If we have

---

[71] Romans 11:29

doubts, we can't receive God's promises. Not so. Doubt is of the flesh, faith is of the Spirit.

The flesh calls us to trust in doubt, and the Spirit gives us faith with the call to believe. Unbelief is when we choose to disbelieve God, even though He has revealed Himself to us. Doubt is nothing more than the call of the flesh. Then Satan confuses Christians by persuading them that because they felt doubt, they are now disqualified from faith.

The truth is, faith destroys doubt. Just as the Bible says that if we walk in the Spirit, we won't fulfill the lusts of the flesh, the same is true for doubt. The lust of the flesh is the intense desire for something that gratifies the flesh. It could be a sexual type of lust, but this is not the only thing the flesh lusts after. It lusts for doubt, for this is the desire to act contrary to the Spirit. It could be the desire for self-righteousness, for this is the flesh's desire to become good without God. Lust is anything the flesh desires in conflict with the life of the Spirit.

Don't fear doubt. Don't fear the emotion of fear. Let faith shield you from these things and rest in the safety of the Spirit. None of these things can force you out of victory. The Bible says, "Let no one rob you of your reward." It is yours by promise. You can only be robbed if you allow it to be taken. If Satan bluffs you into submission, he robs you. But he cannot defeat the one who stands on the promise, "This is the victory that overcomes the world, our faith."

Satan is called the god of this world, so you are already victorious by trusting in Christ's completed work. Satan was disarmed and defeated on the cross. Jesus overcame the world, and you are an overcomer in Him. Or as **Romans 8:37** explains:

Yet in all these things we are more than conquerors through Him who loved us.

Through Christ, you are not merely a conqueror, but more than a conqueror. You have complete victory. Spiritual warfare is standing firm in victory by trusting in God's provisions of grace to us, which is founded upon Christ's victory accomplished for us.

Stand upon Christ victory, and by faith you will do all that is needed to stand. Forget fear. Forget doubt. Forget condemnation. Forget the boastful threats of the enemy. All he can do is either bluff you into surrender, or deceive you into going to war through the flesh. However, those who stand by faith have a victory that cannot be taken.

Discussion Questions

Review 1 John 4:4. Are we trying to overcome the enemy?

What is the difference between a confession of faith and trying to use the power of words?

Review Colossians 3:2-3. Can Satan possess or oppress a life that is hidden in God? Why do people feel oppressed?

Review Romans 7:23-25 and James 1:14. Is temptation an oppression of the devil? How is temptation defeated?

Review 2 Corinthians 10:4-5. If our weapons are not physical, how do we cast down everything that exalts itself against Christ?

Read Romans 12:21. How do we stand against evil? What about politics? What about persecution? What about personal conflicts?

Read Colossians 2:15. If all principalities are disarmed and defeated, what is our role in spiritual warfare?

How is the temptation to resubmit to the law part of our spiritual warfare?

Read Matthew 4:5-7. Will Satan use the scriptures to distract us from faith?

How can we discern when the scriptures are being misused or twisted to miss the mark?

How do we learn to stand in spiritual warfare without falling back into the flesh?

Read Ephesians 6:13. Are we trying to obtain spiritual victory, or holding our position?

Review Romans 8:37. Explain what it means to be more than a conqueror.

Grace is Life in the Spirit

The gospel of grace is a lifestyle of faith. Anyone who teaches a gospel that is dependent upon anything but faith, is teaching a flesh-centered gospel. Anyone who teaches a grace message that is not centered upon Christ is also a flesh-centered gospel.

The gospel of grace is not given to us to comfort us in our sins. It is God's comfort of love that overcomes sin. The Bible gives us the guarantee that where sin abounds, grace MUCH MORE abounds. Grace overcomes sin; it does not teach us to live in sin. Grace is God's declaration that He has taken care of sin, so we can pursue the things of faith without distraction.

Grace renders sin irrelevant. Grace comforts us by revealing the utter defeat of sin through the Spirit's crucifixion of our flesh. The Spirit is not calling us to live in the flesh, but to come out of the flesh. We are not living in the flesh for sin, nor are we living in the flesh for religion or ministry. We are called to live in the Spirit. Look at **Galatians 3:11-14**

> [11] But that no one is justified by the law in the sight of God *is* evident, for "the just shall live by faith."
> [12] Yet the law is not of faith, but "the man who does them shall live by them."
> [13] Christ has redeemed us from the curse of the law, having become a curse for us (for it is written, "Cursed *is* everyone who hangs on a tree "),
> [14] that the blessing of Abraham might come upon the Gentiles in Christ Jesus, that we might receive the promise of the Spirit through faith.

Everything in the Christian life is by faith in what God has provided, not faith in our ability or inability to keep the law. The just shall live by faith. Faith is not merely a moment in time when we believe and receive salvation. Faith is a continuous lifestyle that draws everything from the revelation of our life in the Spirit. Just as Abraham's entire life was built upon walking by faith, ours is too.

Abraham walked in the promise, not knowing how God would meet his needs. When Abraham failed, there were consequences to sin, but God did not deal with him as a sinner, but as a man of promise. The Christian life is a mirror of Abraham's life of promise. We are righteous because God imputed righteousness to us. We journey, not always knowing where we are going or how God will provide. We live by faith, knowing God is for us, and a man or woman of faith doesn't worry about their own inadequacies, for our sufficiency is of God.[72]

Walking in the Spirit is to walk by faith – trusting completely in the love of God. Spiritual maturity is the process of learning how to walk by faith. As we mature, God weans us off of human effort and flesh dependence. No longer will you look to your emotions of the moment to determine if you feel right with God. No longer will you be dependent on sin to feel gratified. No longer will you be dependent upon what you do in order to feel acceptable to God.

I pray that if you take one thing from this book, it is the understanding that everything in the Christian life is the gift of God's grace invested in you. We grow in grace through the knowledge of Christ. The Apostle Paul said, "I have determined not to know anything among you but Jesus Christ, and Him crucified.[73]

This is the consistent teaching of scripture. Legalism is taught by taking scriptures out of context. When scripture is isolated from its context, misconceptions abound. However, we have used many, many scriptures, and these passages have been framed in context. What emerges is the truth that the gospel is what God has done for us through Christ, and the life of faith is learning how to abide in Christ as we learn to trust in His completed work.

We are learning how to receive the work of Christ through the working of the Spirit within us. We are not learning how to make ourselves our own sufficiency. Our faith is not dependent upon our abilities.

People fail when they lose sight of Christ. Those who trust in man's ability to keep the law claim that trusting in grace is

---

[72] 2 Corinthians 3:5
[73] 1 Corinthians 2:2

insufficient, and that believing in grace will lead you into sin. This is not possible, for grace believing is a lifestyle that is focused on Christ. We enter the Spirit by faith, and because grace-living is answering the call to abide in Christ, sin cannot emerge. Sin only emerges when we take our eyes off Christ. Those who are under the law are focused on self, which has already lost focus on Christ.

Yet there will be times when a Christian sins. This is true whether we are under the law, or under grace. We are tempted when we are drawn away through our own lusts and enticed. But there is a difference between the effects of sin under the law and the effects of sin under grace.

When I believed that my sins separated me from God, or broke my fellowship with God, it was hard to climb out of sin. When I stumbled, I would often binge-sin. My spiritual life crumbled, and because I didn't feel accepted, I ran from God until I could get my life right again. There would be times when I would go into a downward spiral until I hit bottom. Then after I had suffered long enough without sinning, I would feel worthy to ask God for forgiveness so I could be accepted again.

What happens to a binge eater who goes into an emotional crisis? What happens when a recovering alcoholic falls off the wagon and feels rotten about himself? They seek comfort in the flesh. The binge eater doesn't just eat a few donuts. They binge until they are sick of food. The alcoholic who falls off the wagon binge drinks until he or she is sick of the bottle.

Yet for some reason, we don't recognize the same is true for other sins. Anger binges on rage. Lust binges on sexual indulgence. Pride binges on self-glorification. When we feel weak in our spirit, we hand the reins over to our flesh.

Grace breaks that curse. When I fully understand that my spiritual life is a gift of God's love, and only His agape love can sustain life, I stop looking to self for sustainability. When I understand that I am 100% acceptable to God because I am in Christ, then when I fall, instead of binging or falling into a downward spiral, I draw strength from my ever-present fellowship with God. Instead of running from God, I run to Him. Instead of fearing His anger, I have the assurance of mercy.

In the Old Testament, when the people were placed under the law, God commanded the people saying that no one was permitted to come near. Anyone who came near the mountain of God when the law was given would be struck down. Anyone who entered the holiest place in the temple, where God dwelled, would be judged and would die.

After Christ fulfilled the law and then took it out of the way, nailing it to the cross,[74] everything changed. Under the law, the command was, "Do not come near lest you die," but under grace after the cross, the command changed to, "Come boldly before the throne of grace when you have need."

Yet Christians are still living as though we are under the curse instead of grace. Because Christ took sin out of the way, and we are in Him, we have the right, the privilege, and the command to come before God's throne without doubt and without fear. This is true even when we sin.

Instead of binging on defeat, grace rescues us the moment we turn to grace. Sin is stopped dead in its tracks and through our unbroken fellowship, God strengthens us. Or should I say, "God becomes our strength." The Bible teaches that we stop falling from a steadfast life in Christ as we learn to grow in grace. Look at **2 Peter 3:17-18**

> [17] You therefore, beloved, since you know *this* beforehand, beware lest you also fall from your own steadfastness, being led away with the error of the wicked;
>
> [18] but grow in the grace and knowledge of our Lord and Savior Jesus Christ. To Him *be* the glory both now and forever. Amen.

This passage follows Peter's warning that in the last days, scoffers will come asking where the promise is of His coming. There are also scoffers in the church asking where is the promise of His coming into our life of faith? People scoff at Christ in many ways.

---

[74] Colossians 2:14

People scoff at the promise that trusting in Christ alone can overcome sin. "Man must do his part," scoffers are proclaiming today. Man's part is found in **John 6:28-29**

> [28] Then they said to Him, "What shall we do, that we may work the works of God?"
>
> [29] Jesus answered and said to them, "This is the work of God, that you believe in Him whom He sent."

Our part is to believe on Jesus. As the Bible says, we have received all things that pertain to life and godliness through Christ. We are not trying to obtain. We are not trying to do. We are learning how to trust in His work and receive all things by faith.

If the Bible says that we have been given all things through Christ, what are we trying to obtain? If the Bible says, "The weakness of the Law was the flesh," which is man's efforts, why would God create a new plan of salvation that was also dependent upon the weakness of man? Where is man's works in this passage, **Romans 4:4-5**

> [4] Now to him who works, the wages are not counted as grace but as debt.
>
> [5] But to him who does not work but believes on Him who justifies the ungodly, his faith is accounted for righteousness,

The Bible then goes on to say that the man of faith has a three-fold blessing. We are blessed because our sins are forgiven.[75] We are blessed because God will not impute sin to us.[76] We are blessed because God imputes His righteousness to us.[77]

But to the one who works, i.e. man does his part, the Bible says, "Your works aren't counted as grace, but as debt." Your works do not earn God's favor, but instead they put you deeper in debt to your sin. Once man believes he has to do his part, grace becomes unattainable.

---

[75] Romans 4:7
[76] Romans 4:8, Romans 5:13
[77] Romans 4:20-25

Grace is Life in the Spirit

According to the scripture in Peter above, how do we become steadfast? We grow in grace and the knowledge of Christ Jesus. The more we discover this lifestyle of grace, the more we become receivers, and because we are walking by faith, our lives become steadfast and immovable from our foundation of righteousness. This is also affirmed in **Colossians 3:9-10**

[9] Do not lie to one another, since you have put off the old man with his deeds,

[10] and have put on the new *man* who is renewed in knowledge according to the image of Him who created him,

Lying is representing the sin of the old man. The man that you have already put off. The old nature is dead and buried, but you can put back on the deeds that the old man produced. If you place your mind in the flesh, this is the natural result. But how do we live as an overcomer?

You have already put on the new man. This is an accomplished fact to any who are born again in Christ. To those who think man must do his part, this passage tells us man's part. To be renewed in knowledge according to the image of Christ. The more you learn of Christ, the more you are renewed, and a renewing life is outgrowing sin. It is not drawn into sin. The more you grow in the knowledge of Christ, the more you are renewed into spiritual maturity, and the less appeal sin has. Growing in knowledge is how we grow in faith.

Faith comes by hearing the word of God,[78] so the more we learn of Christ, the more we learn how to trust in His gift of grace.

We sin because there is a need in our life that we falsely believe sin can fulfill. We can't live in a vacuum. If you take sin away, but never renew in the Spirit, either that same sin or a new sin will fill that void. Sometimes that sin is religious sin. It is man boosting his ego with self-righteousness.

As stated at the beginning of this book, self-righteousness is not only the arrogant person with a judgmental attitude, though it can be. It is also the person who looks holy to the church, but has

---

[78] Romans 10:17

filled their lives with pride-boosting good works instead of the righteousness of God that cannot be earned. From the outside, we cannot judge the heart of another. This is not for us to judge anyone but ourselves. Are WE trying to make ourselves right with God, or are we trusting in the gift of His righteousness?

The needy soul turns to sin in the hope of gratification. The soul that is filled with the Spirit rejects sin, for why would I remove the fruit of the Spirit to replace it with the stench of the flesh? Those who grow in grace through the knowledge of Christ will outgrow sin. As one sin is displaced and buried, God reveals more grace. When we receive these gifts, we then recognize a counterfeit work of the flesh that we must release into God's hands to make room for grace.

Without wrath or fear, the Christian begins to put sins out of their life because they desire something better. This is why the Bible says, "It is the goodness of God that leads you to repentance." We are limited by our own humanity, so it takes time to mature into grace. But as we do, the sins that once seemed too valuable to release become worthless to us. And that is something the law, religion, and self-effort cannot do.

In 2 Corinthians 3, the Bible explains how the law blinds us to grace. The law is called 'The ministry of death,' and is not a reward system, but a condemnation system. Those who study or are taught the law are put under bondage and condemnation, but they are also blinded by the veil of the law. The Bible goes on to explain that this veil is only taken away when we turn to Christ.

Many in the church have reintroduced themselves to the law, and are now blinded by the veil. It is very difficult for them to understand grace, for that veil cannot be taken away until they turn to Christ. We are blind when we look at grace through the lens of the law and claim, "Grace empowers you to keep the law."

But when we believe the Bible's call to trust fully in Christ, who has redeemed us out of the law, put the law to an end, and called us with the promise, "Those who walk in the Spirit are not under the law," then that veil is removed and the scriptures burst with abundant life.

I was one of those Christians. I fought to subdue my flesh, not knowing that it's God's job to suppress my iniquities. I tried to produce righteousness and acceptance, not understanding that these are freely given through Christ, apart from any works. I did not understand that when I tried to become righteous, I was making myself a rival of Jesus. I was shunning the gift of righteousness because I believed I could become righteous by keeping the commandments of the Bible.

When God challenged me through a dear brother, I turned to Christ seeking understanding. The Spirit stirred within me, making me know that something was missing in my perspective. For several weeks I studied grace, praying for God to open my eyes. God drew me into the scriptures, and when the time was come, He took away that veil and all my head knowledge became revelation knowledge. Then the scriptures burst with new life.

That is when I understood that I was veiled from the truth through the law. It's also when I understood the remaining scriptures of **2 Corinthians 3:17-18**

> [17] Now the Lord is the Spirit; and where the Spirit of the Lord *is*, there *is* liberty.
>
> [18] But we all, with unveiled face, beholding as in a mirror the glory of the Lord, are being transformed into the same image from glory to glory, just as by the Spirit of the Lord.

The law puts us under bondage, but the Spirit delivers us into liberty. The veil is removed and now something amazing happens. We take our eyes off the law, and behold the glory given to us through Christ. As we do, we discover that we are being transformed into that same image. The Spirit of the Lord takes the glory of Christ, and begins transforming us into that same glorious image.

And this is what the grace naysayers can't comprehend. We are not outgrowing sin because we make ourselves do so. Nor do we fall back into sin because we stop trying to make ourselves righteous. The Spirit of the Lord does the work. What we could not do under the law – even a Christianized version of the law, the Spirit accomplishes in us.

We are putting our trust in the power of the Spirit, and He transforms us. Grace doesn't make sense to the natural mind because human understanding says, "That can't work. If you take away fear, people will sin." The natural mind says, "Just believing in Christ can't make you righteous. Just trusting in grace can't defeat sin."

True. But it isn't the power of our believing. It is the power of the Spirit. Faith connects us to the Spirit, and when our mind is in the Spirit we become receivers of the Spirit. We have opened the conduits of our heart and mind to the overflowing grace of the Spirit, and then the Spirit transforms our minds. As our mind abides in faith, this flows into our natural life, and sin is rendered impotent.

Sin cannot overcome the Spirit. Sin cannot drive grace out. The flesh cannot exert its power over the Spirit. The flesh is confined to the realm of the flesh, but the Spirit is not confined at all. Yet, God has given us one condition. There is only one thing dependent upon man. Believe. Without faith it is impossible to please God. Without faith it is impossible to live the Christian life.

God has the power to overthrow our will, but God does not. He has made this our one condition for receiving. Keep in mind that faith does not originate from man. The Bible says that God has dealt every person a measure of faith.[79] There is another portion of faith that is given to some as the gifts of the Spirit.[80] Faith is the revelation of God's grace in the Spirit with the invitation to trust God.

The flesh calls out, "That's not enough. Grace is insufficient without man's works." The Spirit calls out, "With man, it is impossible, but with God all things are possible. Only believe."

The flesh says, "Look at your sins. You aren't worthy of grace. You must get it right before you can receive."

---

[79] Romans 12:3
[80] 1 Corinthians 12:9

Grace is Life in the Spirit

The Spirit calls out, "Trust Me. Grace abounds over sin. I will suppress your sins. Your sins are no barrier to My grace. Just believe My word of promise."

God reveals and then calls for us to trust. You can do nothing without Christ. The Spirit gives life. The flesh (human effort) profits nothing.[81] God does not want you to become righteous by your efforts. Look at **2 Corinthians 4:6-7**

> [6] For it is God who commanded light to shine out of darkness, who has shone in our hearts to *give* the light of the knowledge of the glory of God in the face of Jesus Christ.
> [7] But we have this treasure in earthen vessels, that the excellence of the power may be of God and not of us.

The gift of God's grace shines in the darkness of your heart. It shines in the darkness of your flesh. Once the light shines, there is no more darkness, for darkness can't exist in the presence of light. And you have the treasure of God in your earthen vessel. That is your body. You are the temple of God, and the miracle of perfect righteousness and holiness is a gift of God so that He is glorified.

God chose to make the gospel about His grace because He wants you to understand that the glory is a gift of God, and nothing is by us. The power of the excellence of a holy life is meant to show that human effort is irrelevant. The power is of God and not of us. Man doing his part is a denial of grace. It is an attempt of the flesh to steal some of God's glory for selfish pride.

Let's begin wrapping up this book with a passage from **Ephesians 1:17-20**

> [17] that the God of our Lord Jesus Christ, the Father of glory, may give to you the spirit of wisdom and revelation in the knowledge of Him,
> [18] the eyes of your understanding being enlightened; that you may know what is the hope of His calling, what are the riches of the glory of His inheritance in the saints,
> [19] and what *is* the exceeding greatness of His power toward us who believe, according to the working of His mighty

---

[81] John 6:63

power

20 which He worked in Christ when He raised Him from the dead and seated *Him* at His right hand in the heavenly *places*,

The Spirit of wisdom is a gift. It is by revelation in the knowledge of Christ. As you seek to know Christ, He enlightens your understanding, reveals the hope of His calling over you, and you will discover the riches of His glory that is given to you as an inheritance. An inheritance cannot be earned. It is a birthright to those who are children. Everything in the Christian life is God's gift to you. The only things you can give God is your failures and your trust in His grace.

There is one limitation to the exceeding greatness of His power. It is only toward those who believe in the working of His mighty power. The Bible also tells us that the same power that raised Jesus from the dead will give life to your physical bodies.[82] Grace will work in the life of those who believe, for the Spirit has the power to transform your outward behavior through the living power of His Spirit flowing into your inner man.

All God asks of you is to believe. Believe He loves you because He is love. Believe you are forgiven because Jesus bore your sins. Believe the Spirit will transform you as you turn from human effort and behold the glory of Christ. Believe that those who are in Christ have been set free from the law of sin and death. Believe the Bible's promise that Jesus has fulfilled the law of righteousness, and you are credited with God's righteousness solely because you trust in Christ.

Sin is dead. The old man is dead. Reckon yourself dead to sin as you also reckon yourself to be alive in Christ.[83] Reckon, or account this to be true, not because you can measure up, but because God has declared this to be true. It is His gift, received by faith. Then the Holy Spirit begins transforming the lives of those who have the faith to receive this gift that brings glory to God

---

[82] Romans 8:11
[83] Romans 6:11

alone.[84] This is a truth that cannot be seen through the eyes of the flesh, so only those receiving of the Spirit can receive the fullness of God's grace.

You are cherished by God because He is good. God delights in you because you are abiding in Christ. You abide through faith, not works. You are completely accepted because you are in the beloved (Christ).[85]

God did not save you so you could serve Him. God saved you because He is love, and love delights in expressing itself through grace (or unearned favor). As His love flows through our lives, works will emerge, but that is because love delights in expressing itself. As a possessor of God's agape love, we'll begin producing the fruit of agape love.

Love doesn't work because someone demands work, but because it delights in pouring that love into the lives of others. God's desire is to adopt many sons for the purpose of bringing them into His glory.[86] This life has been fashioned for us to know and believe in the love He has for us. Let's close with one final verse, **1 Corinthians 13:13-14:1**

And now abide faith, hope, love, these three; but the
greatest of these *is* love.

When everything is reduced to its basic elements, faith, hope, and love are all that remain. Love is the greatest, for love (agape) is the foundation everything is built upon. God's love is expressed through the Rock of Christ. On the foundation of love, hope is born. Hope is the expectation of God, faith is the assurance that what we hope for is a reality.

God's promises are based on His love for us, and we believe because we know His promise is already a reality waiting to be revealed to those who are receivers.

The enemy attacks our hope and faith by denying God's love. He deceives people into believing that God's love is conditional.

---

[84] Ephesians 1:6
[85] Ephesians 1:6
[86] Hebrews 2:10

The liar says, "If you sin, you lose love. Fellowship is broken and love is cut off. If you don't serve, God won't love you. If you don't love Him enough, He won't love you."

These are all lies. The Bible tells us that the secret of faith is to know and believe in the love God has for us. His perfect love casts out all fear, and even in judgement, we have no fear because we are perfected in God's love. Not our efforts, but God's love.[87]

The one who has a false perception of God's anger or wrath cannot trust God. Someone who fears will never have trust in their tormentor. This is why the enemy works hard to undermine our trust in God's love. However, the one who knows God's love and believes in it has no fear. They only have an expectation of good, and they trust completely in God. As love draws us into deep fellowship, the result can only be transformation into the image of the one we love – who first loved us.[88]

The best part is, we don't have to transform ourselves. We only have to allow the Spirit of love to perform His work in our lives.

Believe God. Trust His word of promise. Walk in faith. The person focused on Christ and is walking by faith (which is complete trust in the work of Christ and His promise to credit us with His work, and transform us into His image) that person IS walking in the Spirit. That person is walking in the law of the Spirit of life in Christ, and has been set free from the law of sin and death.[89]

Know and believe in the unconditional love God has for you, and you'll learn to walk by faith in the life of the Spirit!

---

[87] 1 John 4:16-19
[88] 1 John 4:19
[89] Romans 8:2

Grace is Life in the Spirit

Discussion Questions

What does the Bible mean, "The just shall live by faith?"

When Abraham lied about his wife being his sister to save his own skin, or when he tried to use human effort to produce a child outside of God's provision, did God treat him any different than when he had his act together?

When God worked in Abraham's life to get him out of trouble from his own sin, did this make Abraham more likely to sin?

In Exodus 32:28, God gave Moses the Old Covenant law. 3,000 people died on the day the law was given. In Acts 2:41, when the Spirit gave the New Covenant on the day of Pentecost, 3,000 people were given new life. What does this tell us about the curse of the law verses the gift of grace?

In Exodus 19:12, when God appeared on the mountain, He commanded that the people not come near nor touch the mountain, or else they would die. Read Hebrews 4:15-16. Why are we now commanded to come confidently before God under grace, but were warned not to come near Him under the law?

What prevented people from coming to God in the Old Testament, and what is different in the New Testament?

Review Romans 4:4-5. What makes grace unattainable?

Read Colossians 3:9-10 and 2 Peter 3:17-18. How does a Christian become steadfast in their walk of faith?

Review 2 Corinthians 3:17-18. How are we transformed into the image of Christ?

Read 1 Corinthians 13:4-8, 13. What does this tell you about how God views you when you fail?

The Bible says, "Love keeps no record of wrongs." If this is true, what happens to our sins when it encounters God's love?

Why does the Bible say that out of faith, hope, and love, the greatest of these is love?

Why does Satan focus on making people feel disqualified for God's love?

What do you think it means to walk in the Spirit? Has your understanding changed since you read this question in chapter 1?

Please support this ministry by rating this book on Amazon.com.

Other Recent Books by Eddie Snipes

The Revelation of Grace. Part 1 of this series. God promised to forgive our sins and suppress our iniquities. Discover how God doesn't call us to become holy, but how He defeats sin so we can freely walk in victory.

It is Finished! Step out of condemnation and into the completed work of Christ.

The Promise of a Sound Mind : God's plan for emotional and mental health

Abounding Grace: Dispelling Myths and Clarifying the Biblical Message of God's Overflowing Grace

Other books by Eddie Snipes can be viewed by clicking here.

www.ingramcontent.com/pod-product-compliance
Lightning Source LLC
Chambersburg PA
CBHW061733020426
42331CB00006B/1223